INDIAN HOME RULE

BY

MOHANDAS K. GANDHI

With Bonus Feature

A Letter to a Hindu
The Subjection of India—
Its Cause and Cure

by

Leo Tolstoy

GP

GRINDL PRESS

This edition contains the complete and unabridged manuscripts of *Indian Home Rule*, by M. K. Gandhi and *A Letter to a Hindu*, by Leo Tolstoy. Some obvious typographical errors, however, have been corrected. All content not in the public domain is original to this edition. Content in the public domain includes the manuscript and all images. *Indian Home Rule* originally published in 1922; *A Letter to a Hindu* originally published in 1908.

ISBN: 978-1519642714

GᴵP

GRINDL PRESS
grindlpress.com

from the
Classic Thought
Series
from Grindl Press

Titles of all series from Grindl Press
available for purchase at
www.grindlpress.com

Other Series

Contemporary Editions

Standard Classics

Drama Classics

Classic Short Story Collections

Classic Biography

Mystery Classics

Vocabulary From the Classics

Ethnic Studies

Regional Classics

Old West Classics

American Frontier Series
Classic History

Secondary Student Editions

College Editions

Classic Crafts

Classic Recipes

Classics for Young Adults

Classics for Children

FOREWORD

I have re-read this booklet more than once. The value at the present moment lies in re-printing it as it is. But if I had to revise it, there is only one word I would alter in accordance with a promise made to an English friend. She took exception to my use of the word 'prostitute' in speaking of the Parliament. Her fine taste recoiled from the indelicacy of the expression. I remind the reader that the booklet purports to be a free translation of the original which is in Gujarati.

After years of endeavour to put into practice the views expressed in the following pages, I feel that the way shown therein is the only true way to Swaraj. Satyagrah—the law of love is the Law of life. Departure from it leads to disintegration. A firm adherence to it leads to regeneration.

Bombay,
28th May, 1919
M. K. Gandhi

Hind Swaraj

or

The Indian Home Rule

REPLY TO CRITICS

It is certainly my good fortune that this booklet of mine is receiving wide attention. The original is in Gujarati. It had a chequered career. It was first published in the columns of the 'Indian Opinion' of South Africa. It was written in 1908 during my return voyage from London to South Africa in answer to the Indian school of violence, and its prototype in South Africa. I came in contact with every known Indian anarchist in London. Their bravery impressed me, but I feel that their zeal was misguided. I felt that violence was no remedy for India's ills, and that her civilization required the use of a different and higher weapon for self-protection. The Satyagrah of South Africa was still an infant hardly two years old. But it had developed sufficiently to permit me to write of it with some degree of confidence. It was so much appreciated that it was published as a booklet. It attracted some attention in India. The Bombay Government prohibited its circulation. I replied by publishing its translation. I thought that it was due to my English friends that they should know its contents. In my opinion it is a book which can be put into the hands of a child. It teaches the gospel of love in the place of that of hate. It replaces violence with self-sacrifice. It pits soul force against brute force. It has gone through several editions and I commend it to those who would care to read it. I withdraw nothing except one word of it, and that in deference to a lady friend. I have given the reason for the alteration in the preface to the Indian edition.

The booklet is a severe condemnation of 'modern civilization.' It was written in 1908. My conviction is deeper to-day than ever. I feel that if India would discard 'modern civilization' she can only gain by doing so.

But I would warn the reader against thinking that I am to-day aiming at the Swaraj described therein. I know that India is not ripe for it. It may seem an impertinence to say so. But such is my conviction. I am individually working for the self-rule pictured therein. But to-day my corporate activity is undoubtedly devoted to the attainment of Parliamentary Swaraj in accordance with the wishes of the people of India. I am not aiming at destroying railways or hospitals, though I would certainly welcome their natural destruction. Neither railways nor hospitals are a test of a high and pure civilization. At best they are a necessary evil. Neither adds one inch to the moral stature of a nation. Nor am I aiming at a permanent destruction of law courts, much as I regard it as a 'consummation devoutly to be wished for.' Still less am I trying to destroy all machinery and mills. It requires a higher simplicity and renunciation than the people are to-day prepared for.

The only part of the programme which is now being carried out in its entirety is that of non-violence. But I regret to have to confess that even that is not being carried out in the spirit of the book. If it were, India would establish Swaraj in a day. If India adopted the doctrine of love as an active part of her religion and introduced it in her politics, Swaraj would descend upon India from heaven. But I am painfully aware that that event is far off as yet.

I offer these comments because I observe that much is being quoted from the booklet to discredit the present movement. I have even seen writings suggesting that I am playing a deep game, that I am using the present turmoil to foist my fads on India, and am making religious experiments at India's expense. I can only answer that Satyagrah is made of sterner stuff. There is nothing reserved and nothing secret in it. A portion of the whole theory of life described in 'Hind Swaraj' is undoubtedly being carried into practice. There is no danger attendant upon the whole of it being practised. But it is not right to scare away people by reproducing from my writings passages that are irrelevant to the issue before the country.

M. K. Gandhi,
Young India, 26th January, 1921

CONTENTS

Indian Home Rule

CHAPTER I
THE CONGRESS AND ITS OFFICIALS

READER: Just at present there is a Home Rule wave passing over India. All our countrymen appear to be pining for National Independence. A similar spirit pervades them even in South Africa. Indians seem to be eager after acquiring rights. Will you explain your views in this matter?

EDITOR: You have well put the question, but the answer is not easy. One of the objects of a newspaper is to understand the popular feeling and to give expression to it; another is to arouse among the people certain desirable sentiments; and the third is fearlessly to expose popular defects. The exercise of all these three functions is involved in answering your question. To a certain extent the people's will has to be expressed; certain sentiments will need to be fostered, and defects will have to be brought to light. But, as you have asked the question, it is my duty to answer it.

READER: Do you then consider that a desire for Home Rule has been created among us?

EDITOR: That desire gave rise to the National Congress. The choice of the word "National" implies it.

READER: That, surely, is not the case. Young India seems to ignore the Congress. It is considered to be an instrument for perpetuating British Rule.

EDITOR: That opinion is not justified. Had not the Grand Old Man of India prepared the soil, our young men could not have even spoken about Home Rule. How can we forget what Mr. Hume has written, how he has lashed us into action, and with what effort he has awakened us, in order to achieve the objects of the Congress? Sir William Wedderburn has given his body, mind and money to the same cause. His writings are worthy of perusal to this day. Professor Gokhale, in order to prepare the Nation, embraced poverty and gave twenty years of his life. Even now, he is living in poverty. The late Justice Buddrudin Tyebji was also one of those who, through the Congress, sowed the seed of Home Rule. Similarly in Bengal, Madras, the Punjab and other places, there have been lovers of India and members of the Congress, both Indian and English.

READER: Stay, stay, you are going too far, you are straying away from my question. I have asked you about Home or Self-Rule; you are discussing foreign rule. I do not desire to hear English names, and you are giving me such names. In these circumstances, I do not think we can ever meet. I shall be pleased if you will confine yourself to Home Rule. All other wise talk will not satisfy me.

EDITOR: You are impatient. I cannot afford to be likewise. If you will bear with me for a while, I think you will find that you will obtain what you want. Remember the old proverb that the tree does not grow in one day. The fact that you have checked me, and that you do not want to hear about the well-wishers of India, shows that, for you at any rate, Home Rule is yet far away. If we had many like you, we would never make any advance. This thought is worthy of your attention.

READER: It seems to me that you simply want to put me off by talking round and round. Those whom you consider to be well-wishers of India are not such in my estimation. Why, then, should I listen to your discourse on such people? What has he whom you consider to be the father of the nation done for it? He says that the English Governors will do justice, and that we should co-operate with them.

EDITOR: I must tell you with all gentleness that it must be a matter of shame for us that you should speak about that great man, in terms of disrespect. Just look at his work. He has dedicated his life to the service of India. We have learned what we know from him. It was the respected Dadabhai who taught us that the English had sucked our life-blood.

What does it matter that, to-day, his trust is still in the English nation? Is Dadabhai less to be honoured because, in the exuberance of youth, we are prepared to go a step further? Are we, on that account, wiser than he? It is a mark of wisdom not to kick against the very step from which we have risen higher. The removal of a step from a staircase brings down the whole of it. When, out of infancy we grow into youth, we do not despise infancy, but, on the contrary, we recall with affection the days of our childhood. If, after many years of study, a teacher were to teach me something, and if I were to build a little more on the foundation laid by that teacher, I would not, on that account, be considered wiser than the teacher. He would always command my respect. Such is the case with the Grand Old Man of India. We must admit that he is the author of Nationalism.

READER: You have spoken well. I can now understand that we must look upon Mr. Dadabhai with respect. Without him and men like him, we would probably not have the spirit that fires us. How can the same be said of Professor Gokhale? He has constituted himself a great friend of the English; he says that we have to learn a great deal from them, that we have to learn their political wisdom, before we can talk of Home Rule. I am tired of reading his speeches.

EDITOR: If you are tired, it only betrays your impatience. We believe that those who are discontented with the slowness of their parents, and are angry because the parents would not run with their children, are considered disrespectful to their parents. Professor Gokhale occupies the place of a parent. What does it matter if he cannot run with us? A nation that is desirous of securing Home Rule cannot afford to despise its ancestors. We shall become useless if we lack respect for our elders. Only men with mature thoughts are capable of ruling themselves and not the hasty-tempered. Moreover, how many Indians were there like Professor Gokhale, when he gave himself to Indian education? I verily believe that whatever Professor Gokhale does he does with pure motives and with a view to serving India. His devotion to the Motherland is so great, that he would give his life for it if necessary. Whatever he says is said not to flatter anyone but because he believes it to be true. We are bound, therefore, to entertain the highest regard for him.

READER: Are we, then, to follow him in every respect?

EDITOR: I never said any such thing. If we conscientiously differed from him, the learned Professor himself would advise us to follow the dictates of our conscience rather than him. Our chief purpose is not to cry down his work, but to believe that he is infinitely greater than we, and to feel assured that compared with his work for India, ours is infinitesimal. Several newspapers write disrespectfully of him. It is our duty to protest against such writings. We should consider men like Professor Gokhale to be the pillars of Home Rule. It is a bad habit to say that another man's thoughts are bad and ours only are good, and that those holding different views from ours are the enemies of the country.

READER: I now begin to understand somewhat your meaning. I shall have to think the matter over, but what you say about Mr. Hume and Sir William Wedderburn is beyond comprehension.

EDITOR: The same rule holds good for the English as for the Indians. I can never subscribe to the statement that all Englishmen are bad. Many Englishmen desire Home Rule for India. That the English people are somewhat more selfish than others is true, but that does not prove that every Englishman is bad. We who seek justice will have to do justice to others. Sir William does not wish ill to India—that should be enough for us. As we proceed, you will see that, if we act justly, India will be sooner free. You will see, too, that, if we shun every Englishman as an enemy, Home Rule will be delayed. But if we are just to them, we shall receive their support in our progress towards the goal.

READER: All this seems to me at present to be simply nonsensical. English support and the obtaining of Home Rule are two contradictory things. How can the English people tolerate Home Rule for us? But I do not want you to decide this question for me just yet. To pass time over it is useless. When you have shown how we can have Home Rule, perhaps I shall understand your views. You have prejudiced me against you by discoursing on English help. I would, therefore, beseech you not to continue this subject.

EDITOR: I have no desire to do so. That you are prejudiced against me is not a matter for much anxiety. It is well that I should say unpleasant things at the commencement, it is my duty patiently to try to remove your prejudice.

READER: I like that last statement. It emboldens me to say what I like. One thing still puzzles me. I do not understand how the Congress laid the foundation of Home Rule.

EDITOR: Let us see. The Congress brought together Indians from different parts of India, and enthused us with the idea of Nationality. The Government used to look upon it with disfavour. The Congress has always insisted that the Nation should control revenue and expenditure. It has always desired self-government after the Canadian model. Whether we can get it or not, whether we desire it or not, and whether there is not something more desirable, are different questions. All I have to show is that the Congress gave us a foretaste of Home Rule. To deprive it of the honour is not proper, and for us to do so would not only be ungrateful, but retard the fulfilment of our object. To treat the Congress as an institution inimical to our growth as a Nation would disable us from using that body.

CHAPTER II
THE PARTITION OF BENGAL

READER: Considering the matter as you put it, it seems proper to say that the foundation of Home Rule was laid by the Congress. But you will admit that it cannot be considered a real awakening. When and how did the awakening take place?

EDITOR: The seed is never seen. It works underneath the ground, is itself destroyed, and the tree which rises above the ground is alone seen. Such is the case with the Congress. Yet, what you call the real awakening took place after the Partition of Bengal. For this we have to be thankful to Lord Curzon. At the time of the Partition, the people of Bengal reasoned with Lord Curzon, but, in the pride of power, he disregarded all their prayers—he took it for granted that Indians could only prattle, that they could never take any effective steps. He used insulting language, and, in the teeth of all opposition, partitioned Bengal. That day may be considered to be the day of the partition of the British Empire. The shock that the British power received through the Partition has never been equalled by any other act. This does not mean that the other injustices done to India are less glaring than that done by the Partition. The salt-tax is not a small injustice. We shall see many such things later on. But the people were ready to resist the Partition. At that time, the feeling ran high. Many leading Bengalis were ready to lose their all. They knew their power; hence the conflagration. It is now well nigh unquenchable; it is not necessary to quench it either. Partition will go, Bengal will be re-united, but the rift in the English barque will remain: it must daily widen. India awakened is not likely to fall asleep. Demand for abrogation of Partition is tantamount to demand for Home Rule. Leaders in Bengal know this, British officials realise it. That is why Partition still remains. As time passes, the Nation is being forged. Nations are not formed in a day; the formation requires years.

READER: What, in your opinion, are the results of Partition?

EDITOR: Hitherto we have considered that for redress of grievances, we must approach the Throne and, if we get no redress, we must sit still, except that we may still petition. After the Partition, people saw that petitions must be backed up by force, and that they must be capable of suffering. This new spirit must be considered to be the chief result of Partition. That spirit was seen in the outspoken writings in the press. That which the people said tremblingly and in secret began to be said and to be written publicly. The Swadeshi movement was inaugurated. People, young and old, used to run away at the sight of an English face; it now no longer awed them. They did not fear even a row, or being imprisoned. Some of the best sons of India are at present in banishment. This is something different from mere petitioning. Thus are the people moved. The spirit generated in Bengal has spread in the North to the Punjab, and in the South to Cape Comorin.

READER: Do you suggest any other striking result?

EDITOR: The Partition has not only made a rift in the English ship, but has made it in ours also. Great events always produce great results. Our leaders are divided into two parties: the Moderates and the Extremists. These may be considered as the slow party and the impatient party. Some call the Moderates the timid party, and the Extremists the bold party. All interpret the two words according to their pre-conceptions. This much is certain—that there has arisen an enmity between the two. The one distrusts the other, and imputes motives. At the time of the Surat Congress, there was almost a fight. I think that this division is not a good thing for the country, but I think also that such divisions will not last long. It all depends upon the leaders how long they will last.

CHAPTER III
DISCONTENT AND UNREST

READER: Then you consider Partition to be a cause of the awakening? Do you welcome the unrest which has resulted from it?

EDITOR: When a man rises from sleep, he twists his limbs and is restless. It takes some time before he is entirely awakened. Similarly, although the Partition has caused an awakening, the comatose has not yet disappeared. We are still twisting our limbs and still restless, and just as the state between sleep and awakening must be considered to be necessary, so may the present unrest in India be considered a necessary and, therefore, a proper state. The knowledge that there is unrest will, it is highly probable, enable us to outgrow it. Rising from sleep, we do not continue in a comatose state, but, according to our ability, sooner or later, we are completely restored to our senses. So shall we be free from the present unrest which no one likes.

READER: What is the other form of unrest?

EDITOR: Unrest is, in reality, discontent. The latter is only now described as unrest. During the Congress-period it was labelled discontent; Mr. Hume always said that the spread of discontent in India was necessary. This discontent is a very useful thing. So long as a man is contented with his present lot, so long is it difficult to persuade him to come out of it. Therefore it is that every reform must be preceded by discontent. We throw away things we have only when we cease to like them. Such discontent has been produced among us after reading the great works of Indians and Englishmen. Discontent has led to unrest, and the latter has brought about many deaths, many imprisonments, many banishments. Such a state of things will still continue. It must be so. All these may be considered good signs, but they may also lead to bad results.

Chapter IV
What is Swaraj?

READER: I have now learnt what the Congress has done to make India one nation, how the Partition has caused an awakening, and how discontent and unrest have spread through the land. I would now like to know your views on Swaraj. I fear that our interpretation is not the same.

EDITOR: It is quite possible that we do not attach the same meaning to the term. You and I and all Indians are impatient to obtain Swaraj, but we are certainly not decided as to what it is. To drive the English out of India is a thought heard from many mouths, but it does not seem that many have properly considered why it should be so. I must ask you a question. Do you think that it is necessary to drive away the English, if we get all we want?

READER: I should ask of them only one thing that is: "Please leave our country." If after they have complied with this request, their withdrawal from India means that they are still in India, I should have no objection. Then we would understand that, in our language, the word "gone" is equivalent to "remained."

EDITOR: Well then, let us suppose that the English have retired. What will you do then?

READER: That question cannot be answered at this stage. The state after withdrawal will depend largely upon the manner of it. If, as you assume, they retire, it seems to me we shall still keep their constitution, and shall carry on the government. If they simply retire for the asking, we should have an army, etc. ready at hand. We should, therefore, have no difficulty in carrying on the government.

EDITOR: You may think so: I do not. But I will not discuss the matter just now. I have to answer your question, and that I can do well by asking you several questions. Why do you want to drive away the English?

READER: Because India has become impoverished by their government. They take away our money from year to year. The most important posts are reserved for themselves. We are kept in a state of slavery. They behave insolently towards us, and disregard our feelings.

EDITOR: If they do not take our money away, become gentle, and give us responsible posts, would you still consider their presence to be harmful?

READER: That question is useless. It is similar to the question whether there is any harm in associating with a tiger, if he changes his nature. Such a question is sheer waste of time. When a tiger changes his nature, Englishmen will change theirs. This is not possible, and to believe it to be possible is contrary to human experience.

EDITOR: Supposing we get self-government similar to what the Canadians and the South Africans have, will it be good enough?

READER: That question also is useless. We may get it when we have the same powers; we shall then hoist our own flag. As is Japan, so must India be. We must own our navy, our army, and we must have our own splendour, and then will India's voice ring through the world.

EDITOR: You have well drawn the picture. In effect it means this: that we want English rule without the Englishman. You want the tiger's nature, but not the tiger; that is to say, you would make India English, and when it becomes English, it will be called not Hindustan but Englistan. This is not the Swaraj that I want.

READER: I have placed before you my idea of Swaraj as I think it should be. If the education we have received be of any use, if the works of Spencer, Mill and others be of any importance and if the English

Parliament be the mother of Parliaments, I certainly think that we should copy the English people and this to such an extent that, just as they do not allow others to obtain a footing in their country, so we should not allow them or others to obtain it in ours. What they have done in their own country has not been done in any other country. It is, therefore, proper for us to import their institutions. But now I want to know your views.

EDITOR: There is need for patience. My views will develop of themselves in the course of this discourse. It is as difficult for me to understand the true nature of Swaraj as it seems to you to be easy. I shall, therefore, for the time being, content myself with endeavouring to show that what you call Swaraj is not truly Swaraj.

CHAPTER V
THE CONDITION OF ENGLAND

READER: Then from your statement, I deduce the Government of England is not desirable and not worth copying by us.

EDITOR: Your deduction is justified. The condition of England at present is pitiable. I pray to God that India may never be in that plight. That which you consider to be the Mother of Parliaments is like a sterile woman and a prostitute. Both these are harsh terms, but exactly fit the case. That Parliament has not yet of its own accord done a single good thing, hence I have compared it to a sterile woman. The natural condition of that Parliament is such that, without outside pressure, it can do nothing. It is like a prostitute because it is under the control of ministers who change from time to time. To-day it is under Mr. Asquith, to-morrow it may be under Mr. Balfour.

READER: You have said this sarcastically. The term "sterile woman" is not applicable. The Parliament, being elected by the people, must work under public pressure. This is its quality.

EDITOR: You are mistaken. Let us examine it a little more closely. The best men are supposed to be elected by the people. The members serve without pay and, therefore, it must be assumed only for the public weal. The electors are considered to be educated and, therefore, we should assume that they would not generally make mistakes in their choice. Such a Parliament should not need the spur of petitions or any other pressure. Its work should be so smooth that its effect would be more apparent day by day. But, as a matter of fact, it is generally acknowledged that the members are hypocritical and selfish. Each thinks of his own little interest. It is fear that is the guiding motive. What is done to-day may be undone to-morrow. It is not possible to recall a single instance in which the finality can be predicted for its work. When the greatest questions are debated its members have been seen to stretch themselves and to doze. Sometimes the members talk away until the listeners are disgusted. Carlyle has called it the "talking shop of the world." Members vote for their party without a thought. Their so-called discipline binds them to it. If any member, by way of exception, gives an independent vote, he is considered a renegade. If the money and the time wasted by the Parliament were entrusted to a few good men, the English nation would be occupying to-day a much higher platform. The Parliament is simply a costly toy of the nation. These views are, by no means, peculiar to me. Some great English thinkers have expressed them. One of the members of the Parliament recently said that a true Christian could not become a member of it. Another said that it was a baby. And, if it has remained a baby after an existence of seven hundred years, when will it outgrow its babyhood?

READER: You have set me thinking; you do not expect me to accept at once all you say. You give me entirely novel views. I shall have to digest them. Will you now explain the epithet "prostitute"?

EDITOR: That you cannot accept my views at once is only right. If you will read the literature on this subject, you will have some idea of it. The Parliament is without a real master. Under the Prime Minister, its movement is not steady, but it is buffeted about like a prostitute. The Prime Minister is more concerned about his power than about the welfare of the Parliament. His energy is concentrated upon securing the success of his party. His care is not always that the Parliament shall do right. Prime Ministers are known to have made the Parliament do things merely for party advantage. All this is worth thinking over.

READER: Then you are really attacking the very men whom we have hitherto considered to be patriotic and honest?

EDITOR: Yes, that is true; I can have nothing against Prime Ministers, but what I have seen leads me to think that they cannot be considered really patriotic. If they are to be considered honest because they do not take what is generally known as bribery, let them be so considered, but they are open to subtler influences. In order to gain their ends, they certainly bribe people with honours. I do not hesitate to say that they have neither real honesty nor a living conscience.

READER: As you express these views about the Parliament, I would like to hear you on the English people, so that I may have your views of their Government.

EDITOR: To the English voters their newspaper is their Bible. They take cue from their newspapers, which latter are often dishonest. The same fact is differently interpreted by different newspapers, according to the party in whose interests they are edited. One newspaper would consider a great Englishman to be a paragon of honesty, another would consider him dishonest. What must be the condition of the people whose newspapers are of this type?

READER: You shall describe it.

EDITOR: These people change their views frequently. It is said that they change them every seven years. These views swing like the pendulum of a clock and are never steadfast. The people would follow a powerful orator or a man who gives them parties, receptions, etc. As are the people, so is their Parliament. They have certainly one quality very strongly developed. They will never allow their country to be lost. If any person were to cast an evil eye on it, they would pluck out his eyes. But that does not mean that the nation possesses every other virtue or that it should be imitated. If India copies England, it is my firm conviction that she will be ruined.

READER: To what do you ascribe this state of England?

EDITOR: It is not due to any peculiar fault of the English people, but the condition is due to modern civilization. It is a civilization only in name. Under it the nations of Europe are becoming degraded and ruined day by day.

CHAPTER VI
CIVILIZATION

READER: Now you will have to explain what you mean by civilization.

EDITOR: It is not a question of what I mean. Several English writers refuse to call that, civilization which passes under that name. Many books have been written upon that subject. Societies have been formed to cure the nation of the evils of civilization. A great English writer has written a work called "Civilization: Its Cause and Cure." Therein he has called it a disease.

READER: Why do we not know this generally?

EDITOR: The answer is very simple. We rarely find people arguing against themselves. Those who are intoxicated by modern civilization are not likely to write against it. Their care will be to find out facts and arguments in support of it, and this they do unconsciously, believing it to be true. A man, whilst he is dreaming, believes in his dream; he is undeceived only when he is awakened from his sleep. A man labouring under the bane of civilization is like a dreaming man. What we usually read are the work of defenders of modern civilization, which undoubtedly claims among its votaries very brilliant and even some very good men. Their writings hypnotise us. And so, one by one, we are drawn into the vortex.

READER: This seems to be very plausible. Now will you tell me something of what you have read and thought of this civilization.

EDITOR: Let us first consider what state of things is described by the word "civilization." Its true test lies in the fact that people living in it make bodily welfare the object of life. We will take some examples. The people of Europe to-day live in better-built houses than they did a hundred years ago. This is considered an emblem of civilization, and this is also a matter to promote bodily happiness. Formerly, they wore skins, and used as their weapons spears. Now, they wear long trousers, and for embellishing their bodies they wear a variety of clothing, and, instead of spears, they carry with them revolvers containing five or more chambers. If people of a certain country, who have hitherto not been in the habit of wearing much clothing, boots, etc., adopt European clothing, they are supposed to have become civilised out of savagery. Formerly, in Europe, people ploughed their lands mainly by manual labour. Now, one man can plough a vast tract by means of steam-engines, and can thus amass great wealth. This is called a sign of civilization. Formerly, the fewest men wrote books, that were most valuable. Now, anybody writes and prints anything he likes and poisons people's minds. Formerly, men travelled in waggons; now they fly through the air, in trains at the rate of four hundred and more miles per day. This is considered the height of civilization. It has been stated that, as men progress, they shall be able to travel in airships and reach any part of the world in a few hours. Men will not need the use of their hands and feet. They will press a button, and they will have their clothing by their side. They will press another button, and they will have their newspaper. A third, and a motor-car will be in waiting for them. They will have a variety of delicately dished up food. Everything will be done by machinery. Formerly, when people wanted to fight with one another, they measured between them their bodily strength; now it is possible to take away thousands of lives by one man working behind a gun from a hill. This is civilization. Formerly, men worked in the open air only so much as they liked. Now, thousands of workmen meet together and for the sake of maintenance work in factories or mines. Their condition is worse than that of beasts. They are obliged to work, at the risk of their lives, at most dangerous occupations, for the sake of millionaires. Formerly, men were made slaves under physical compulsion, now they are enslaved by temptation of money and of the luxuries that money can buy. There are now diseases of which people never dreamt before, and an army of doctors is engaged in finding out their cures, and so hospitals have increased. This is a test of civilization. Formerly, special messengers were required and much expense was incurred in order to send letters; to-day, anyone can abuse his fellow by means of a letter for one penny. True, at the same cost, one can send one's thanks also. Formerly, people had two or three meals consisting of homemade bread and vegetables; now, they require something to eat every two hours, so that they have hardly leisure for anything else. What more need I say? All this you can ascertain from several authoritative books. These are all true tests of civilization. And, if any one speaks to the contrary, know that he is ignorant. This civilization takes note neither of morality nor of religion. Its votaries calmly state that their business is not to teach religion. Some even consider it to be a superstitious growth. Others put on the cloak of religion, and prate about morality. But, after twenty years' experience, I have come to the conclusion that immorality is often taught in the name of morality. Even a child can understand that in all I have described above there can be no inducement to morality. Civilization seeks to increase bodily comforts, and it fails miserably even in doing so.

This civilization is irreligion, and it has taken such a hold on the people in Europe that those who are in it appear to be half mad. They lack real physical strength or courage. They keep up their energy by intoxication. They can hardly be happy in solitude. Women, who should be the queens of households, wander in the streets, or they slave away in factories. For the sake of a pittance, half a million women in England alone are labouring under trying circumstances in factories or similar institutions. This awful fact is one of the causes of the daily growing suffragette movement.

This civilization is such that one has only to be patient and it will be self-destroyed. According to the teaching of Mahomed this would be considered a Satanic civilization. Hinduism calls it the Black Age. I cannot give you an adequate conception of it. It is eating into the vitals of the English nation. It must be shunned. Parliament are really emblems of slavery. If you will sufficiently think over this, you will entertain the same opinion, and cease to blame the English. They rather deserve our sympathy. They are a shrewd nation and I therefore believe that they will cast off the evil. They are enterprising and industrious and their mode of thought is not inherently immoral. Neither are they bad at heart. I, therefore, respect them. Civilization is not an incurable disease, but it should never be forgotten that the English people are at present afflicted by it.

Chapter VII
Why was India Lost?

READER: You have said much about civilization—enough to make me ponder over it. I do not now know what I should adopt and what I should avoid from the nations of Europe, but one question comes to my lips immediately. If civilization is a disease, and if it has attacked England why has she been able to take India, and why is she able to retain it?

EDITOR: Your question is not very difficult to answer, and we shall presently be able to examine the true nature of Swaraj; for I am aware that I have still to answer that question. I will, however, take up your previous question. The English have not taken India; we have given it to them. They are not in India because of their strength, but because we keep them. Let us now see whether these propositions can be sustained. They came to our country originally for purposes of trade. Recall the Company Bahadur. Who made it Bahadur? They had not the slightest intention at the time of establishing a kingdom. Who assisted the Company's officers? Who was tempted at the sight of their silver? Who bought their goods? History testifies that we did all this. In order to become rich all at once, we welcomed the Company's officers with open arms. We assisted them. If I am in the habit of drinking Bhang and a seller thereof sells it to me, am I to blame him or myself? By blaming the seller shall I be able to avoid the habit? And, if a particular retailer is driven away, will not another take his place? A true servant of India will have to go to the root of the matter. If an excess of food has caused me indigestion, I will certainly not avoid it by blaming water. He is a true physician who probes the cause of disease and, if you pose as a physician for the disease of India, you will have to find out its true cause.

READER: You are right. Now, I think you will not have to argue much with me to drive your conclusions home. I am impatient to know your further views. We are now on a most interesting topic. I shall, therefore, endeavour to follow your thought, and stop you when I am in doubt.

EDITOR: I am afraid that, in spite of your enthusiasm, as we proceed further we shall have differences of opinion. Nevertheless, I shall argue only when you will stop me. We have already seen that the English merchants were able to get a footing in India because we encouraged them. When our princes fought among themselves, they sought the assistance of Company Bahadur. That corporation was versed alike in commerce and war. It was unhampered by questions of morality. Its object was to increase its commerce, and to make money. It accepted our assistance, and increased the number of its warehouses. To protect the latter it employed an army which was utilised by us also. Is it not then useless to blame the English for what we did at that time? The Hindus and the Mahomedans were at daggers drawn. This, too, gave the Company its opportunity; and thus we created the circumstances that gave the Company its control over India. Hence it is truer to say that we gave India to the English than that India was lost.

READER: Will you now tell me how they are able to retain India?

EDITOR: The causes that gave them India enable them to retain it. Some Englishmen state that they took, and they hold, India by the sword. Both these statements are wrong. The sword is entirely useless for holding India. We alone keep them. Napoleon is said to have described the English as a nation of shop-keepers. It is a fitting description. They hold whatever dominions they have for the sake of their commerce. Their army and their navy are intended to protect it. When the Transvaal offered no such attractions, the late Mr. Gladstone discovered that it was not right for the English to hold it. When it became a paying proposition, resistance led to war. Mr. Chamberlain soon discovered that England enjoyed a suzerainty over the Transvaal. It is related that some one asked the late President Kruger whether there was gold in the moon. He replied that it was highly unlikely, because, if there were, the English would have annexed it. Many problems can be solved by remembering that money is their God. Then it follows that we keep the English in India for our base self-interest. We like their commerce, they please us by their subtle methods, and get what they want from us. To blame them for this is to perpetuate their power. We further strengthen their hold by quarrelling amongst ourselves. If you accept the above statements, it is proved that the English entered India for the purposes of trade. They remain in it for the same purpose, and we help them to do so. Their arms and ammunition are perfectly useless. In this connection, I remind you that it is the British flag which is waving in Japan, and not the Japanese. The English have a treaty with Japan for the sake of their commerce, and you will see that, if they can manage it, their commerce will greatly expand in that country. They wish to convert the whole world into a vast market for their goods. That they cannot do so is true, but the blame will not be theirs. They will leave no stone unturned to reach the goal.

CHAPTER VIII
THE CONDITION OF INDIA

READER: I now understand why the English hold India. I should like to know your views about the condition of our country.

EDITOR: It is a sad condition. In thinking of it, my eyes water and my throat get parched. I have grave doubts whether I shall be able sufficiently to explain what is in my heart. It is my deliberate opinion that India is being ground down not under the English heel but under that of modern civilization. It is groaning under the monster's terrible weight. There is yet time to escape it, but every day makes it more and more difficult. Religion is dear to me, and my first complaint is that India is becoming irreligious. Here I am not thinking of the Hindu and Mahomedan or the Zoroastrian religion, but of the religion which underlies all religions. We are turning away from God.

READER: How so?

EDITOR: There is a charge laid against us that we are a lazy people, and that the Europeans are industrious and enterprising. We have accepted the charge and we, therefore, wish to change our condition. Hinduism, Islamism, Zoroastrianism, Christianity and all other religions teach that we should remain passive about worldly pursuits and active about godly pursuits, that we should set a limit to our worldly ambition, and that our religious ambition should be illimitable. Our activity should be directed into the latter channel.

READER: You seem to be encouraging religious charlatanism. Many a cheat has by talking in a similar strain led the people astray.

EDITOR: You are bringing an unlawful charge against religion.

Humbug there undoubtedly is about all religions. Where there is light, there is also shadow. I am prepared to maintain that humbugs in worldly matters are far worse than the humbugs in religion. The humbug of civilization that I endeavour to show to you is not to be found in religion.

READER: How can you say that? In the name of religion Hindus and Mahomedans fought against one another. For the same cause Christians fought Christians. Thousands of innocent men have been murdered, thousands have been burned and tortured in its name. Surely, this is much worse than any civilization.

EDITOR: I certainly submit that the above hardships are far more bearable than those of civilization. Everybody understands that the cruelties you have named are not part of religion, although they have been practised in its name: therefore there is no aftermath to these cruelties. They will always happen so long as there are to be found ignorant and credulous people. But there is no end to the victims destroyed in the fire of civilization. Its deadly effect is that people came under its scorching flames believing it to be all good. They become utterly irreligious and, in reality, derive little advantage from the world. Civilization is like a mouse gnawing, while it is soothing us. When its full effect is realised, we will see that religious superstition is harmless compared to that of modern civilization. I am not pleading for a continuance of religious superstitions. We will certainly fight them tooth and nail, but we can never do so by disregarding religion. We can only do so by appreciating and conserving the latter.

READER: Then you will contend that the Pax Britannica is a useless encumbrance?

EDITOR: You may see peace if you like; I see none.

READER: You make light of the terror that Thugs, the Pindaris, the Bhils were to the country.

EDITOR: If you will give the matter some thought, you will see that the terror was by no means such a mighty thing. If it had been a very substantial thing, the other people would have died away before the

English advent. Moreover, the present peace is only nominal, for by it we have become emasculated and cowardly. We are not to assume that the English have changed the nature of the Pindaris and the Bhils. It is, therefore, better to suffer the Pindari peril than that some one else should protect us from it, and thus render us effeminate. I should prefer to be killed by the arrow of a Bhil than to seek unmanly protection. India without such protection was an India full of valour. Macaulay betrayed gross ignorance when he libelled Indians as being practically cowards. They never merited the charge. Cowards living in a country inhabited by hardy mountaineers, infested by wolves and tigers must surely find an early grave. Have you ever visited our fields? I assure you that our agriculturists sleep fearlessly on their farms even to-day, and the English, you and I would hesitate to sleep where they sleep. Strength lies in absence of fear, not in the quantity of flesh and muscle we may have on our bodies. Moreover, I must remind you who desire Home Rule that, after all, the Bhils, the Pindaris, the Assamese and the Thugs are our own countrymen. To conquer them is your and my work. So long as we fear our own brethren, we are unfit to reach the goal.

CHAPTER IX
THE CONDITION OF INDIA (CONTINUED)

RAILWAYS

READER: You have deprived me of the consolation I used to have regarding peace in India.

EDITOR: I have merely given you my opinion on the religious aspect, but when I give you my views as to the poverty of India you will perhaps begin to dislike me, because what you and I have hitherto considered beneficial for India no longer appears to me to be so.

READER: What may that be?

EDITOR: Railways, lawyers and doctors have impoverished the country, so much so that, if we do not wake up in time, we shall be ruined.

READER: I do now indeed fear that we are not likely to agree at all. You are attacking the very institutions which we have hitherto considered to be good.

EDITOR: It is necessary to exercise patience. The true inwardness of the evils of civilization you will understand with difficulty. Doctors assure us that a consumptive clings to life even when he is about to die. Consumption does not produce apparent hurt—it even produces a seductive colour about a patient's face, so as to induce the belief that all is well. Civilization is such a disease, and we have to be very wary.

READER: Very well, then, I shall hear you on the railways.

EDITOR: It must be manifest to you that, but for the railways, the English could not have such a hold on India as they have. The railways, too, have spread the bubonic plague. Without them, masses could not move from place to place. They are the carriers of plague germs. Formerly we had natural segregation. Railways have also increased the frequency of famines, because, owing to facility of means of locomotion, people sell out their grain, and it is sent to the dearest markets. People become careless, and so the pressure of famine increases. They accentuate the evil nature of man. Bad men fulfil their evil designs with greater rapidity. The holy places of India have become unholy. Formerly people went to these places with very great difficulty. Generally, therefore, only the real devotees visited such places. Now-a-days, rogues visit them in order to practise their roguery.

READER: You have given an one-sided account. Good men can visit these places as well as bad men. Why do they not take the fullest advantage of the railways?

EDITOR: Good travels at a snail's pace—it can, therefore, have little to do with the railways. Those who want to do good are not selfish, they are not in a hurry, they know that to impregnate people with good requires a long time. But evil has wings. To build a house takes time. Its destruction takes none. So the railways can become a distributing agency for the evil one only. It may be a debatable matter whether railways spread famines, but it is beyond dispute that they propagate evil.

READER: Be that as it may, all the disadvantages of railways are more than counter-balanced by the fact that it is due to them that we see in India the new spirit of nationalism.

EDITOR: I hold this to be a mistake. The English have taught us that we were not one nation before, and that it will require centuries before we become one nation. This is without foundation. We were one nation before they came to India. One thought inspired us. Our mode of life was the same. It was because we were one nation that they were able to establish one kingdom. Subsequently they divided us.

READER: This requires an explanation.

EDITOR: I do not wish to suggest that because we were one nation we had no differences, but it is submitted that our leading men travelled throughout India either on foot or in bullock-carts. They learned one another's languages, and there was no aloofness between them. What do you think could have been the intention of those far-seeing ancestors of ours who established Shethubindu-Rameshwar in the South, Juggernaut in the South-East and Hardwar in the North as places of pilgrimage? You will admit they were no fools. They knew that worship of God could have been performed just as well at home. They taught us that those whose hearts were aglow with righteousness had the Ganges in their own homes. But they saw that India was one undivided land so made by nature. They, therefore, argued that it must be one nation. Arguing thus, they established holy places in various parts of India, and fired the people with an idea of nationality in a manner unknown in other parts of the world. Any two Indians are one as no two Englishmen are. Only you and I and others who consider ourselves civilised and superior persons imagine that we are many nations. It was after the advent of railways that we began to believe in distinctions, and you are at liberty now to say that it is through the railways that we are beginning to abolish those distinctions. An opium-eater may argue the advantage of opium-eating from the fact that he began to understand the evil of the opium habit after having eaten it. I would ask you to consider well what I have said on the railways.

READER: I will gladly do so, but one question occurs to me even now. You have described to me the India of the pre-Mahomedan period, but now we have Mahomedans, Parsees and Christians. How can they be one nation? Hindus and Mahomedans are old enemies. Our very proverbs prove it. Mahomedans turn to the West for worship whilst Hindus turn to the East. The former look down on the Hindus as idolators. The Hindus worship the cow, the Mahomedans kill her. The Hindus believe in the doctrine of non-killing, the Mahomedans do not. We thus meet with differences at every step. How can India be one nation?

CHAPTER X
THE CONDITION OF INDIA (CONTINUED)

THE HINDUS AND THE MAHOMEDANS

EDITOR: Your last question is a serious one; and yet, on careful consideration, it will be found to be easy of solution. The question arises because of the presence of the railways, of the lawyers and of the doctors. We shall presently examine the last two. We have already considered the railways. I should, however, like to add that man is so made by nature as to require him to restrict his movements as far as his hands and feet will take him. If we did not rush about from place to place by means of railways and such other maddening conveniences, much of the confusion that arises would be obviated. Our difficulties are of our own creation. God set a limit to a man's locomotive ambition in the construction of his body. Man immediately proceeded to discover means of overriding the limit. God gifted man with intellect that he might know his Maker. Man abused it, so that he might forget his Maker. I am so constructed that I can only serve my immediate neighbours, but in my conceit, I pretend to have discovered that I must with my body serve every individual in the Universe. In thus attempting the impossible, man comes in contact with different natures, different religions and is utterly confounded. According to this reasoning, it must be apparent to you that railways are a most dangerous institution. Man has there through gone further away from his Maker.

READER: But I am impatient to hear your answer to my question. Has the introduction of Mahomedanism not unmade the nation?

EDITOR: India cannot cease to be one nation because people belonging to different religions live in it. The introduction of foreigners does not necessarily destroy the nation, they merge in it. A country is one nation only when such a condition obtains in it. That country must have a faculty for assimilation. India has ever been such a country. In reality, there are as many religions as there are individuals, but those who are conscious of the spirit of nationality do not interfere with one another's religion. If they do, they are not fit to be considered a nation. If the Hindus believe that India should be peopled only by Hindus, they are living in dreamland. The Hindus, the Mahomedans, the Parsees and the Christians who have made India their country are fellow-countrymen, and they will have to live in unity if only for their own interest. In no part of the world are one nationality and one religion synonymous terms; nor has it ever been so in India.

READER: But what about the inborn enmity between Hindus and Mahomedans?

EDITOR: That phrase has been invented by our mutual enemy. When the Hindus and Mahomedans fought against one another, they certainly spoke in that strain. They have long since ceased to fight. How, then, can there be any inborn enmity? Pray remember this too, that we did not cease to fight only after British occupation. The Hindus flourished under Moslem sovereigns and Moslems under the Hindu. Each party recognised that mutual fighting was suicidal, and that neither party would abandon its religion by force of arms. Both parties, therefore, decided to live in peace. With the English advent the quarrels re-commenced.

The proverbs you have quoted were coined when both were fighting; to quote them now is obviously harmful. Should we not remember that many Hindus and Mahomedans own the same ancestors, and the same blood runs through their veins? Do people become enemies because they change their religion? Is the God of the Mahomedan different from the God of the Hindu? Religions are different roads converging to the same point. What does it matter that we take different roads, so long as we reach the same goal? Wherein is the cause for quarrelling?

Moreover, there are deadly proverbs as between the followers of Shiva and those of Vishnu, yet nobody suggests that these two do not belong to the same nation. It is said that the Vedic religion is different from Jainism, but the followers of the respective faiths are not different nations. The fact is that we have become enslaved, and, therefore, quarrel and like to have our quarrels decided by a third party. There are Hindu iconoclasts as there are Mahomedan. The more we advance in true knowledge, the better we shall understand that we need not be at war with those whose religion we may not follow.

READER: Now I would like to know your views about cow protection.

EDITOR: I myself respect the cow, that is I look upon her with affectionate reverence. The cow is the protector of India, because, it being an agricultural country, is dependant on the cow's progeny. She is a most useful animal in hundreds of ways. Our Mahomedan brethren will admit this.

But, just as I respect the cow so do I respect my fellow-men. A man is just as useful as a cow, no matter whether he be a Mahomedan or a Hindu. Am I, then, to fight with or kill a Mahomedan in order to save a cow? In doing so, I would become an enemy as well of the cow as of the Mahomedan. Therefore, the only method I know of protecting the cow is that I should approach my Mahomedan brother and urge him for the sake of the country to join me in protecting her. If he would not listen to me, I should let the cow go for the simple reason that the matter is beyond my ability. If I were over full of pity for the cow, I should sacrifice my life to save her, but not take my brother's. This, I hold, is the law of our religion.

When men become obstinate, it is a difficult thing. If I pull one way, my Moslem brother will pull another. If I put on a superior air, he will return the compliment. If I bow to him gently, he will do it much more so, and if he does not, I shall not be considered to have done wrong in having bowed. When the Hindus became insistent, the killing of cows increased. In my opinion, cow protection societies may be considered cow-killing societies. It is a disgrace to us that we should need such societies. When we forgot how to protect cows, I suppose we needed such societies.

What am I to do when a blood-brother is on the point of killing a cow? Am I to kill him, or to fall down at his feet and implore him? If you admit that I should adopt the latter course, I must do the same to my Moslem brother.

Who protects the cow from destruction by Hindus when they cruelly ill-treat her? Whoever reasons with the Hindus when they mercilessly belabour the progeny of the cow with their sticks? But this has not prevented us from remaining one nation.

Lastly, if it be true that the Hindus believe in the doctrine of non-killing and the Mahomedans do not, what, I pray, is the duty of the former? It is not written that a follower of the religion of Ahimsa (non-killing) may kill a fellow-man. For him the way is straight. In order to save one being, he may not kill another. He can only plead—therein lies his sole duty.

But does every Hindu believe in Ahimsa? Going to the root of the matter, not one man really practises such a religion, because we do destroy life. We are said to follow that religion because we want to obtain freedom from liability to kill any kind of life. Generally speaking, we may observe that many Hindus partake of meat and are not, therefore, followers of Ahimsa. It is, therefore, preposterous to suggest that the two cannot live together amicably because the Hindus believe in Ahimsa and the Mahomedans do not.

These thoughts are put into our minds by selfish and false religious teachers. The English put the finishing touch. They have a habit of writing history; they pretend to study the manners and customs of all peoples. God has given us a limited mental capacity, but they usurp the function of the God-head and indulge in novel experiments. They write about their own researches in most laudatory terms and hypnotise us into believing them. We, in our ignorance, then fall at their feet.

Those who do not wish to misunderstand things may read up the Koran, and will find therein hundreds of passages acceptable to the Hindus; and the Bhagavad-Gita contains passages to which not a Mahomedan can take exception. Am I to dislike a Mahomedan because there are passages in the Koran I do not understand or like? It takes two to make a quarrel. If I do not want to quarrel with a Mahomedan, the latter will be powerless to foist a quarrel on me, and, similarly, I should be powerless if a Mahomedan refuses his assistance to quarrel with me. An arm striking the air will become disjointed. If every one will try to understand the core of his own religion and adhere to it, and will not allow false teachers to dictate to him, there will be no room left for quarrelling.

READER: But will the English ever allow the two bodies to join hands?

EDITOR: This question arises out of your timidity. It betrays our shallowness. If two brothers want to live in peace is it possible for a third party to separate them? If they were to listen to evil counsels, we would consider them to be foolish. Similarly, we Hindus and Mahomedans would have to blame our folly rather than the English, if we allowed them to put us asunder. A claypot would break through impact; if not with one stone, then with another. The way to save the pot is not to keep it away from the danger point, but to bake it so that no stone would break it. We have then to make our hearts of perfectly baked clay. Then we shall be steeled against all danger. This can be easily done by the Hindus. They are superior in numbers, they pretend that they are more educated, they are, therefore, better able to shield themselves from attack on their amicable relations with the Mahomedans.

There is mutual distrust between the two communities. The Mahomedans, therefore, ask for certain concessions from Lord Morley. Why should the Hindus oppose this? If the Hindus desisted, the English would notice it, the Mahomedans would gradually begin to trust the Hindus, and brotherliness would be the outcome. We should be ashamed to take our quarrels to the English. Everyone can find out for himself that the Hindus can lose nothing by desisting. That man who has inspired confidence in another has never lost anything in this world.

I do not suggest that the Hindus and the Mahomedans will never fight. Two brothers living together often do so. We shall sometimes have our heads broken. Such a thing ought not to be necessary, but all men are not equiminded. When people are in a rage, they do many foolish things. These we have to put up with. But, when we do quarrel, we certainly do not want to engage counsel and to resort to English or any law-courts. Two men fight; both have their heads broken, or one only. How shall a third party distribute justice amongst them? Those who fight may expect to be injured.

CHAPTER XI
THE CONDITION OF INDIA (CONTINUED)

LAWYERS

READER: You tell me that, when two men quarrel, they should not go to a law-court. This is astonishing.

EDITOR: Whether you call it astonishing or not, it is the truth. And your question introduces us to the lawyers and the doctors. My firm opinion is that the lawyers have enslaved India and they have accentuated the Hindu-Mahomedan dissensions, and have confirmed English authority.

READER: It is easy enough to bring these charges, but it will be difficult for you to prove them. But for the lawyers, who would have shown us the road to independence? Who would have protected the poor? Who would have secured justice? For instance, the late Mr. Manomohan Ghose defended many a poor man free of charge. The Congress, which you have praised so much, is dependent for its existence and activity upon the work of the lawyers. To denounce such an estimable class of men is to spell justice injustice, and you are abusing the liberty of the press by decrying lawyers.

EDITOR: At one time I used to think exactly like you. I have no desire to convince you that they have never done a single good thing. I honour Mr. Ghose's memory. It is quite true that he helped the poor. That the Congress owes the lawyers something is believable. Lawyers are also men, and there is something good in every man. Whenever instances of lawyers having done good can be brought forward, it will be found that the good is due to them as men rather than as lawyers. All I am concerned with is to show you that the profession teaches immorality; it is exposed to temptations from which few are saved.

The Hindus and the Mahomedans have quarrelled. An ordinary man will ask them to forget all about it, he will tell them that both must be more or less at fault, and will advise them no longer to quarrel. They go to lawyers. The latter's duty is to side with their clients, and to find out ways and arguments in favour of the clients to which they (the clients) are often strangers. If they do not do so, they will be considered to have degraded their profession. The lawyers, therefore, will, as a rule advance quarrels, instead of repressing them. Moreover, men take up that profession, not in order to help others out of their miseries, but to enrich themselves. It is one of the avenues of becoming wealthy and their interest exists in multiplying disputes. It is within my knowledge that they are glad when men have disputes. Petty pleaders actually manufacture them. Their touts, like so many leeches, suck the blood of the poor people. Lawyers are men who have little to do. Lazy people, in order to indulge in luxuries, take up such professions. This is a true statement. Any other argument is a mere pretension. It is the lawyers who have discovered that theirs is an honourable profession. They frame laws as they frame their own praises. They decide what fees they will charge, and they put on so much side that poor people almost consider them to be heaven-born. Why do they want more fees than common labourers? Why are their requirements greater? In what way are they more profitable to the country than the labourers? Are those who do good entitled to greater payment? And, if they have done anything for the country for the sake of money, how shall it be counted as good?

Those who know anything of the Hindu-Mahomedan quarrels know that they have been often due to the intervention of lawyers. Some families have been ruined through them; they have made brothers enemies. Principalities, having come under lawyer's power, have become loaded with debt. Many have been robbed of their all. Such instances can be multiplied.

But the greatest injury they have done to the country is that they have tightened the English grip. Do you think that it would be possible for the English to carry on their government without law-courts? It is wrong to consider that courts are established for the benefit of the people. Those who want to perpetuate their power do so through the courts. If people were to settle their own quarrels, a third party would not be able to exercise any authority over them. Truly, men were less unmanly when they settled their disputes either by fighting or by asking their relatives to decide upon them. They became more unmanly and cowardly when they resorted to the courts of law. It was certainly a sign of savagery when they settled their disputes by fighting. Is it any the less so if I ask a third party to decide between you and me? Surely, the decision of a third party is not always right. The parties alone know who is right. We, in our simplicity and ignorance, imagine that a stranger, by taking our money, gives us justice.

The chief thing, however, to be remembered is that, without lawyers, courts could not have been established or conducted, and without the latter the English could not rule. Supposing that there were only English Judges, English Pleaders and English Police, they could only rule over the English. The English could not do without Indian Judges and Indian pleaders. How the pleaders were made in the first instance and how they were favoured you should understand well. Then you will have the same abhorrence for the profession that I have. If pleaders were to abandon their profession, and consider it just as degrading as prostitution, English rule would break up in a day. They have been instrumental in having the charge laid against us that we love quarrels and courts, as fish love water. What I have said with reference to the pleaders necessarily applies to the judges; they are first cousins, and the one gives strength to the other.

CHAPTER XII

THE CONDITION OF INDIA (CONTINUED)

DOCTORS

READER: I now understand the lawyers; the good they may have done is accidental. I feel that the profession is certainly hateful. You, however, drag in these doctors also, how is that?

EDITOR: The views I submit to you are those I have adopted. They are not original. Western writers have used stronger terms regarding both lawyers and doctors. One writer has likened the whole modern system to the Upas tree. Its branches are represented by parasitical professions, including those of law and medicine, and over the trunk has been raised the axe of true religion. Immorality is the root of the tree. So you will see that the views do not come right out of my mind, but they represent the combined experiences of many. I was at one time a great lover of the medical profession. It was my intention to become a doctor for the sake of the country. I no longer hold that opinion. I now understand why the medicine men (the vaids) among us have not occupied a very honourable status.

The English have certainly effectively used the medical profession for holding us. English physicians are known to have used the profession with several Asiatic potentates for political gain.

Doctors have almost unhinged us. Sometimes I think that quacks are better than highly qualified doctors. Let us consider: the business of a doctor is to take care of the body, or, properly speaking, not even that. Their business is really to rid the body of diseases that may afflict it. How do these diseases arise? Surely by our negligence or indulgence. I overeat, I have indigestion, I go to a doctor, he gives me medicine. I am cured, I overeat again, and I take his pills again. Had I not taken the pills in the first instance, I would have suffered the punishment deserved by me, and I would not have overeaten again. The doctor intervened and helped me to indulge myself. My body thereby certainly felt more at ease, but my mind became weakened. A continuance of a course of a medicine must, therefore, result in loss of control over the mind.

I have indulged in vice, I contract a disease, a doctor cures me, the odds are that I shall repeat the vice. Had the doctor not intervened, nature would have done its work, and I would have acquired mastery over myself, would have been freed from vice, and would have become happy.

Hospitals are institutions for propagating sin. Men take less care of their bodies, and immorality increases. European doctors are the worst of all. For the sake of a mistaken care of the human body, they kill annually thousands of animals. They practise vivisection. No religion sanctions this. All say that it is not necessary to take so many lives for the sake of our bodies.

These doctors violate our religious instinct. Most of their medical preparations contain either animal fat or spirituous liquors; both of these are tabooed by Hindus and Mahomedans. We may pretend to be civilised, call religious prohibitions a superstition and wantonly indulge in what we like. The fact remains that the doctors induce us to indulge, and the result is that we have become deprived of self-control and have become effeminate. In these circumstances, we are unfit to serve the country. To study European medicine is to deepen our slavery.

It is worth considering why we take up the profession of medicine. It is certainly not taken up for the purpose of serving humanity. We become doctors so that we may obtain honours and riches. I have endeavoured to show that there is no real service of humanity in the profession, and that it is injurious to mankind. Doctors make a show of their knowledge, and charge exorbitant fees. Their preparations, which are intrinsically worth a few pennies, cost shillings. The populace in its credulity and in the hope of ridding itself of some disease, allows itself to be cheated. Are not quacks then, whom we know, better than the doctors who put on an air of humaneness?

CHAPTER XIII
WHAT IS TRUE CIVILIZATION?

READER: You have denounced railways, lawyers and doctors. I can see that you will discard all machinery. What, then, is civilization?

EDITOR: The answer to that question is not difficult. I believe that the civilization India has evolved is not to be beaten in the world. Nothing can equal the seeds sown by our ancestors. Rome went, Greece shared the same fate, the might of the Pharaohs was broken, Japan has become westernised, of China nothing can be said, but India is still, somehow or other, sound at the foundation. The people of Europe learn their lessons from the writings of the men of Greece or Rome, which exist no longer in their former glory. In trying to learn from them, the Europeans imagine that they will avoid the mistakes of Greece and Rome. Such is their pitiable condition. In the midst of all this, India remains immovable, and that is her glory. It is a charge against India that her people are so uncivilised, ignorant and stolid, that it is not possible to induce them to adopt any changes. It is a charge really against our merit. What we have tested and found true on the anvil of experience, we dare not change. Many thrust their advice upon India, and she remains steady. This is her beauty; it is the sheet-anchor of our hope.

Civilization is that mode of conduct which points out to man the path of duty. Performance of duty and observance of morality are convertible terms. To observe morality is to attain mastery over our mind and our passions. So doing, we know ourselves. The Gujarati equivalent for civilization means "good conduct."

If this definition be correct, then India, as so many writers have shown, has nothing to learn from anybody else, and this is as it should be. We notice that mind is a restless bird; the more it gets the more it wants, and still remains unsatisfied. The more we indulge our passions, the more unbridled they become. Our ancestors, therefore, set a limit to our indulgences. They saw that happiness was largely a mental condition. A man is not necessarily happy because he is rich, or unhappy because he is poor. The rich are often seem to be unhappy, the poor to be happy. Millions will always remain poor. Observing all this, our ancestors dissuaded us from luxuries and pleasures. We have managed with the same kind of plough as it existed thousands of years ago. We have retained the same kind of cottages that we had in former times, and our indigenous education remains the same as before. We have had no system of life-corroding competition. Each followed his own occupation or trade, and charged a regulation wage. It was not that we did not know how to invent machinery, but our forefathers knew that, if we set our hearts after such things, we would become slaves and lose our moral fibre. They, therefore, after due deliberation, decided that we should only do what we could with our hands and feet. They saw that our real happiness and health consisted in a proper use of our hands and feet. They further reasoned that large cities were a snare and a useless encumbrance, and that people would not be happy in them, that there would be gangs of thieves and robbers, prostitution and vice flourishing in them, and that poor men would be robbed by rich men. They were, therefore, satisfied with small villages. They saw that kings and their swords were inferior to the sword of ethics, and they, therefore, held the sovereigns of the earth to be inferior to the Rishis and the Fakirs. A nation with a constitution like this is fitter to teach others than to learn from others. This nation had courts, lawyers and doctors, but they were all within bounds. Everybody knew that these professions were not particularly superior; moreover, these vakils and vaids did not rob people; they were considered people's dependents, not their masters. Justice was tolerably fair. The ordinary rule was to avoid courts. There were no touts to lure people into them. This evil, too, was noticeable only in and around capitals. The common people lived independently, and followed their agricultural occupation. They enjoyed true Home Rule.

And where this cursed modern civilization has not reached, India remains as it was before. The inhabitants of that part of India will very properly laugh at your new-fangled notions. The English do not rule over them nor will you ever rule over them. Those whose name we speak we do not know, nor do they know us. I would certainly advise you and those like you who love the motherland to go into the interior that has yet not been polluted by the railways, and to live there for six months; you might then be patriotic and speak of Home Rule.

Now you see what I consider to be real civilization. Those who want to change conditions such as I have described are enemies of the country and are sinners.

READER: It would be all right if India were exactly as you have described it; but it is also India where there are hundreds of child-widows, where two-year-old babies are married, where twelve-year-old girls are mothers and housewives, where women practise polyandry, where the practice of Niyog obtains, where, in the name of religion, girls dedicate themselves to prostitution, and where, in the name of religion, sheep and goats are killed. Do you consider these also symbols of the civilization that you have described?

EDITOR: You make a mistake. The defects that you have shown are defects. Nobody mistakes them for ancient civilization. They remain in spite of it. Attempts have always been made, and will be made, to remove them. We may utilise the new spirit that is born in us for purging ourselves of these evils. But what I have described to you as emblems of modern civilization are accepted as such by its votaries. The Indian civilization, as described by me, has been so described by its votaries. In no part of the world, and under no civilization, have all men attained perfection. The tendency of Indian civilization is to elevate the moral being, that of the western civilization is to propagate immorality. The latter is godless, the former is based on a belief in God. So understanding and so believing, it behoves every lover of India to cling to the old Indian civilization even as a child clings to its mother's breast.

Chapter XIV
How Can India Become Free?

READER: I appreciate your views about civilization. I will have to think over them. I cannot take in all at once. What, then, holding the views you do, would you suggest for freeing India?

EDITOR: I do not expect my views to be accepted all of a sudden. My duty is to place them before readers like yourself. Time can be trusted to do the rest. We have already examined the conditions for freeing India, but we have done so indirectly; we will now do so directly. It is a world-known maxim that the removal of the cause of a disease results in the removal of the disease itself. Similarly, if the cause of India's slavery be removed, India can become free.

READER: If Indian civilization is, as you say, the best of all, how do you account for India's slavery?

EDITOR: This civilization is unquestionably the best; but it is to be observed that all civilizations have been on their trial. That civilization which is permanent outlives it. Because the sons of India were found wanting, its civilization has been placed in jeopardy. But its strength is to be seen in its ability to survive the shock. Moreover, the whole of India is not touched. Those alone who have been affected by western civilization have become enslaved. We measure the universe by our own miserable foot-rule. When we are slaves, we think that the whole universe is enslaved. Because we are in an abject condition, we think that the whole of India is in that condition. As a matter of fact, it is not so, but it is as well to impute our slavery to the whole of India. But if we bear in mind the above fact we can see that, if we become free, India is free. And in this thought you have a definition of Swaraj. It is Swaraj when we learn to rule ourselves. It is therefore in the palm of our hands. Do not consider this Swaraj to be like a dream. Hence there is no idea of sitting still. The Swaraj that I wish to picture before you and me is such that, after we have once realised it, we will endeavour to the end of our lifetime to persuade others to do likewise. But such Swaraj has to be experienced by each one for himself. One drowning man will never save another. Slaves ourselves, it would be a mere pretension to think of freeing others. Now you will have seen that it is not necessary for us to have as our goal the expulsion of the English. If the English become Indianised, we can accommodate them. If they wish to remain in India along with their civilization, there is no room for them. It lies with us to bring about such a state of things.

READER: It is impossible that Englishmen should ever become Indianised.

EDITOR: To say that is equivalent to saying that the English have no humanity in them. And it is really beside the point whether they become so or not. If we keep our own house in order, only those who are fit to live in it will remain. Others will leave of their own accord. Such things occur within the experience of all of us.

READER: But it has not occurred in history!

EDITOR: To believe that, what has not occurred in history will not occur at all, is to argue disbelief in the dignity of man. At any rate, it behoves us to try what appeals to our reason. All countries are not similarly conditioned. The condition of India is unique. Its strength is immeasurable. We need not, therefore, refer to the history of other countries. I have drawn attention to the fact that, when other civilizations have succumbed, the Indians has survived many a shock.

READER: I cannot follow this. There seems little doubt that we shall have to expel the English by force of arms. So long as they are in the country, we cannot rest. One of our poets says that slaves cannot even dream of happiness. We are, day by day, becoming weakened owing to the presence of the English. Our greatness is gone; our people look like terrified men. The English are in the country like a blight which we must remove by every means.

EDITOR: In your excitement, you have forgotten all we have been considering. We brought the English, and we keep them. Why do you forget that our adoption of their civilization makes their presence in India at all possible? Your hatred against them ought to be transferred to their civilization. But let us assume that we have to drive away the English by fighting; how is that to be done?

READER: In the same way as Italy did it. What it was possible for Mazzini and Garibaldi to do, is possible for us. You cannot deny that they were very great men.

CHAPTER XV

ITALY AND INDIA

EDITOR: It is well that you have instanced Italy. Mazzini was a great and good man; Garibaldi was a great warrior. Both are adorable; from their lives we can learn much. But the condition of Italy was different from that of India. In the first instance the difference between Mazzini and Garibaldi is worth noting. Mazzini's ambition was not, and has not yet been realised, regarding Italy. Mazzini has shown in his writings on the duty of man that every man must learn how to rule himself. This has not happened in Italy. Garibaldi did not hold this view of Mazzini's. Garibaldi gave, and every Italian took arms. Italy and Austria had the same civilization; they were cousins in this respect. It was a matter of tit for tat. Garibaldi simply wanted Italy to be free from the Austrian yoke. The machinations of Minister Cavour disgrace that portion of the history of Italy. And what has been the result? If you believe that, because Italians rule Italy, the Italian nation is happy, you are groping in darkness. Mazzini has shown conclusively that Italy did not become free. Victor Emanuel gave one meaning to the expression; Mazzini gave another. According to Emanuel, Cavour, and even Garibaldi, Italy meant the King of Italy and his henchmen. According to Mazzini, it meant the whole of the Italian people, that is, its agriculturists. Emanuel was only its servant. The Italy of Mazzini still remains in a state of slavery. At the time of the so-called national war, it was a game of chess between two rival kings, with the people of Italy as pawns. The working classes in that land are still unhappy. They therefore indulge in assassination, rise in revolt, and rebellion on their part is always expected. What substantial gain did Italy obtain after the withdrawal of the Austrian troops? The gain was only nominal. The reforms, for the sake of which the war was supposed to have been undertaken, have not yet been granted. The condition of the people, in general, still remains the same. I am sure you do not wish to reproduce such a condition in India. I believe that you want the millions of India to be happy, not that you want the reins of Government in your hands. If that be so, we have to consider only one thing: how can the millions obtain self-rule? You will admit that people under several Indian princes are being ground down. The latter mercilessly crush them. Their tyranny is greater than that of the English, and, if you want such tyranny in India, that we shall never agree. My patriotism does not teach me that I am to allow people to be crushed under the heel of Indian princes, if only the English retire. If I have the power, I should resist the tyranny of Indian princes just as much as that of the English. By patriotism I mean the welfare of the whole people, and, if I could secure it at the hands of the English, I should bow down my head to them. If any Englishman dedicated his life to securing the freedom of India, resisting tyranny and serving the land, I should welcome that Englishman as an Indian.

Again, India can fight like Italy only when she has arms. You have not considered this problem at all. The English are splendidly armed; that does not frighten me, but it is clear that, to fit ourselves against them in arms, thousands of Indians must be armed. If such a thing be possible, how many years will it take. Moreover, to arm India on a large scale is to Europeanise it. Then her condition will be just as pitiable as that of Europe. This means, in short, that India must accept European civilization, and if that is what we want, the best thing is that we have among us those who are so well trained in that civilization. We will then fight for a few rights, will get what we can and so pass our days. But the fact is that the Indian nation will not adopt arms, and it is well that it does not.

READER: You are overassuming facts. All need not be armed. At first, we will assassinate a few Englishmen and strike terror; then a few men who will have been armed will fight openly. We may have to lose a quarter of a million men, more or less, but we will regain our land. We will undertake guerilla warfare, and defeat the English.

EDITOR: That is to say, you want to make the holy land of India unholy. Do you not tremble to think of freeing India by assassination? What we need to do is to kill ourselves. It is a cowardly thought, that of killing others. Whom do you suppose to free by assassination? The millions of India do not desire it. Those who are intoxicated by the wretched modern civilization think of these things. Those who will rise to power by murder will certainly not make the nation happy. Those who believe that India has gained by Dhingra's act and such other acts in India make a serious mistake. Dhingra was a patriot, but his love was blind. He gave his body in a wrong way; its ultimate result can only be mischievous.

READER: But you will admit that the English have been frightened by these murders, and that Lord Morley's reforms are due to fear.

EDITOR: The English are both a timid and a brave nation. She is, I believe, easily influenced by the use of gunpowder. It is possible that Lord Morley has granted the reforms through fear, but what is granted under fear can be retained only so long as the fear lasts.

CHAPTER XVI
BRUTE-FORCE

READER: This is a new doctrine; that what is gained through fear is retained only while the fear lasts. Surely, what is given will not be withdrawn?

EDITOR: Not so. The Proclamation of 1857 was given at the end of a revolt, and for the purpose of preserving peace. When peace was secured and people became simple-minded, its full effect was toned down. If I ceased stealing for fear of punishment, I would re-commence the operation so soon as the fear is withdrawn from me. This is almost a universal experience. We have assumed that we can get men to do things by force and, therefore, we use force.

READER: Will you not admit that you are arguing against yourself? You know that what the English obtained in their own country they have obtained by using brute-force. I know you have argued that what they have obtained is useless, but that does not affect my argument. They wanted useless things, and they got them. My point is that their desire was fulfilled. What does it matter what means they adopted? Why should we not obtain our goal which is good, by any means whatsoever even by using violence? Shall I think of the means when I have to deal with a thief in the house? My duty is to drive him out anyhow. You seem to admit that we have received nothing, and that we shall receive nothing by petitioning. Why, then, may we not do so by using brute-force? And, to retain what we may receive, we shall keep up the fear by using the same force to the extent that it may be necessary. You will not find fault with a continuance of force to prevent a child from thrusting its foot into fire? Somehow or other, we have to gain our end.

EDITOR: Your reasoning is plausible. It has deluded many. I have used similar arguments before now. But I think I know better now, and I shall endeavour to undeceive you. Let us first take the argument that we are justified in gaining our end by using brute-force, because the English gained theirs by using similar means. It is perfectly true that they used brute-force, and that it is possible for us to do likewise: but by using similar means, we can get only the same thing that they got. You will admit that we do not want that. Your belief that there is no connection between the means and the end is a great mistake. Through that mistake even men who have been considered religious have committed grievous crimes. Your reasoning is the same as saying that we can get a rose through planting a noxious weed. If I want to cross the ocean, I can do so only by means of a vessel; if I were to use a cart for that purpose, both the cart and I would soon find the bottom. "As is the God, so is the votary," is a maxim worth considering. Its meaning has been distorted, and men have gone astray. The means may be likened to a seed, the end to a tree; and there is just the same inviolable connection between the means and the end as there is between the seed and the tree. I am not likely to obtain the result flowing from the worship of God by laying myself prostrate before Satan. If, therefore, anyone were to say: "I want to worship God: it does not matter that I do so by means of Satan," it would be set down as ignorant folly. We reap exactly as we sow. The English in 1833 obtained greater voting power by violence. Did they, by using brute-force, better appreciate their duty? They wanted the right of voting, which they obtained by using physical-force. But real rights are a result of performance of duty; these rights they have not obtained. We, therefore, have before us in England the force of everybody wanting and insisting on his rights, nobody thinking of his duty. And, where everybody wants rights, who shall give them and to whom? I do not wish to imply that they never perform their duty, but I do wish to imply that they do not perform the duty to which those rights should correspond; and, as they do not perform that particular duty, namely, acquire fitness, their rights have proved a burden to them. In other words, what they have obtained is an exact result of the means they adopted. They used the means corresponding to the end. If I want to deprive you of your watch, I shall certainly have to fight for it; if I want to buy your watch, I shall have to pay you for it; and, if I want a gift, I shall have to plead for it; and, according to the means I employ, the watch is stolen property, my own property, or a donation. Thus we see three different results from three different means. Will you still say that means do not matter?

Now we shall take the example given by you of the thief to be driven out. I do not agree with you that the thief may be driven out by any means. If it is my father who has come to steal I shall use one kind of means. If it is an acquaintance, I shall use another; and, in the case of a perfect stranger, I shall use a third. If it is a white man, you will perhaps say, you will use means different from those you will adopt with an Indian thief. If it is a weakling, the means will be different from those to be adopted for dealing with an equal in physical strength; and, if the thief is armed from tip to toe, I shall simply remain quiet. Thus we have a variety of means between the father and the armed man. Again, I fancy that I should pretend to be sleeping whether the thief was my father or that strong-armed man. The reason for this is that my father would also be armed, and I should succumb to the strength possessed by either, and allow my things to be stolen. The strength of my father would make me weep with pity; the strength of the armed man would rouse in me anger, and we should become enemies. Such is the curious situation. From these examples, we may not be able to agree as to the means to be adopted in each case. I myself seem clearly to see what should be done in all these cases, but the remedy may frighten you. I, therefore, hesitate to place it before you. For the time being, I will leave you to guess it, and, if you cannot, it is clear that you will have to adopt different means in each case. You will also have seen that any means will not avail to drive away the thief. You will have to adopt means to fit each case. Hence it follows that your duty is *not* to drive away the thief by any means you like.

Let us proceed a little further. That a well-armed man has stolen your property, you have harboured the thought, you are filled with anger; you argue that you want to punish that rogue, not for your own sake, but for the good of your neighbours; you have collected a number of armed men, you want to take his house by assault, he is duly informed of it, he runs away; he too, is incensed. He collects his brother-robbers, and sends you a defiant message that he will commit robbery in broad day-light. You are strong, you do not fear him, you are prepared to receive him. Meanwhile, the robber pesters your neighbours. They complain before you, you reply that you are doing all for their sake; you do not mind that your own goods have been stolen. Your neighbours reply that the robber never pestered them before, and that he commenced his depredations only after you declared hostilities against him. You are between Sylla and Charybdis. You are full of pity for the poor men. What they say is true. What are you to do? You will be disgraced if you now leave the robber alone. You, therefore, tell the poor men: "Never mind. Come, my wealth is yours, I will give you arms, I will teach you how to use them; you should belabour the rogue; don't you leave him alone." And so the battle grows; the robbers increase in number; your neighbours have deliberately put themselves to inconvenience. Thus the result of wanting to take revenge upon the robber is that you have disturbed your own peace; you are in perpetual fear of being robbed and assaulted; your courage has given place to cowardice. If you will patiently examine the argument, you will see that I have not overdrawn the picture. This is one of the means. Now let us examine the other. You set this armed robber down as an ignorant brother; you intend to reason with him at a suitable opportunity; you argue that he is, after all, a fellow-man; you do not know what prompted him to steal. You, therefore, decide that, when you can, you will destroy the man's motive for stealing. Whilst you are thus reasoning with yourself, the man comes again to steal. Instead of being angry with him, you take pity on him. You think that this stealing habit must be a disease with him. Henceforth you, therefore, keep your doors and windows open; you change your sleeping-place, and you keep your things in a manner most accessible to him. The robber comes again, and is confused, as all this is new to him; nevertheless, he takes away your things. But his mind is agitated. He inquires about you in the village, he comes to learn about your broad and loving heart, he repents, he begs your pardon, returns you your things, and leaves off the stealing habit. He becomes your servant, and you find for him honourable employment. This is the second method. Thus, you see different means have brought about totally different results. I do not wish to deduce from this that robbers will act in the above manner or that all will have the same pity and love like you; but I wish only to show that only fair means can produce fair results, and that, at least in the majority of cases, if not, indeed, in all, the force of love and pity is infinitely greater than the force of arms. There is harm in the exercise of brute-force, never in that of pity.

Now we will take the question of petitioning. It is a fact beyond dispute that a petition, without the backing of force, is useless. However, the late Justice Ranade used to say that petitions served a useful purpose because they were a means of educating people. They give the latter an idea of their condition, and warn the rulers. From this point of view, they are not altogether useless. A petition of an equal is a sign of courtesy; a petition from a slave is a symbol of his slavery. A petition backed by force is a petition from an equal and, when he transmits his demand in the form of a petition, it testifies to his nobility. Two kinds of force can back petitions. "We will hurt you if you do not give this" is one kind of force; it is the force of arms, whose evil results we have already examined. The second kind of force can thus be stated: "If you do not concede our demand, we will be no longer your petitioners. You can govern us only so long as we remain the governed; we shall no longer have any dealings with you." The force implied in this may be described as love-force, soul-force, or, more popularly but less accurately, passive resistance. This force is indestructible. He who uses it perfectly understands his position. We have an ancient proverb which literally means "One negative cures thirty-six diseases." The force of arms is powerless when matched against the force of love or the soul.

Now we shall take your last illustration, that of the child thrusting its foot into fire. It will not avail you. What do you really do to the child? Supposing that it can exert so much physical force that it renders you powerless and rushes into fire, then you cannot prevent it. There are only two remedies open to you—either you must kill it in order to prevent it from perishing in the flames, or you must give your own life, because you do not wish to see it perish before your very eyes. You will not kill it. If your heart is not quite full of pity, it is possible that you will not surrender yourself by preceding the child and going into the fire yourself.

You, therefore, helplessly allow it to go into the flames. Thus, at any rate, you are not using physical force. I hope you will not consider that it is still physical-force, though of a low order, when you would forcibly prevent the child from rushing towards the fire if you could. That force is of a different order, and we have to understand what it is.

Remember that, in thus preventing the child, you are minding entirely its own interest, you are exercising authority for its sole benefit. Your example does not apply to the English. In using brute-force against the English, you consult entirely your own, that is the national interest. There is no question here either of pity or of love. If you say that the actions of the English, being evil, represent fire, and that they proceed to their actions through ignorance, and that, therefore, they occupy the position of a child, and that you want to protect such a child, then you will have to overtake every such evil action by whomsoever committed, and, as in the case of the child, you will have to sacrifice yourself. If you are capable of such immeasurable pity, I wish you well in its exercise.

CHAPTER XVII
PASSIVE RESISTANCE

READER: Is there any historical evidence as to the success of what you have called soul-force or truth-force? No instance seems to have happened of any nation having risen through soul-force. I still think that the evil-doers will not cease doing evil without physical punishment.

EDITOR: The poet Tulsidas has said: "Of religion, pity or love is the root, as egotism of the body. Therefore, we should not abandon pity so long as we are alive." This appears to me to be a scientific truth. I believe in it as much as I believe in two and two being four. The force of love is the same as the force of the soul or truth. We have evidence of its working at every step. The universe would disappear without the existence of that force. But you ask for historical evidence. It is, therefore, necessary to know what history means. The Gujarati equivalent means: "It so happened." If that is the meaning of history, it is possible to give copious evidence. But if it means the doings of kings and emperors, there can be no evidence of soul-force or passive resistance in such history. You cannot expect silver-ore in a tin-mine. History, as we know it, is a record of the wars of the world, and so there is a proverb among Englishmen that a nation which has no history, that is, no wars, is a happy nation. How kings played how they become enemies of one another and how they murdered one another is found accurately recorded in history and, if this were all that had happened in the world, it would have been ended long ago. If the story of the universe had commenced with wars, not a man would have been found alive to-day. Those people who have been warred against have disappeared, as, for instance, the natives of Australia, of whom hardly a man was left alive by the intruders. Mark, please, that these natives did not use soul-force in self-defence, and it does not require much foresight to know that the Australians will share the same fate as their victims. "Those that wield the sword shall perish by the sword." With us, the proverb is that professional swimmers will find a watery grave.

The fact that there are so many men still alive in the world shows that it is based not on the force of arms but on the force of truth or love. Therefore the greatest and most unimpeachable evidence of the success of this force is to be found in the fact that, in spite of the wars of the world, it still lives on.

Thousands, indeed, tens of thousands, depend for their existence on a very active working of this force. Little quarrels of millions of families in their daily lives disappear before the exercise of this force. Hundreds of nations live in peace. History does not and cannot take note of this fact. History is really a record of every interruption of the even working of the force of love or of the soul. Two brothers quarrel: one of them repents and re-awakens the love that was lying dormant in him; the two again begin to live in peace: nobody takes note of this. But if the two brothers, through the intervention of solicitors or some other reason, take up arms or go to law—which is another form of the exhibition of brute-force— their doings would be immediately noticed in the press, they would be the talk of their neighbours, and would probably go down to history. And what is true of families and communities is true of nations. There is no reason, to believe that there is one law for families, and another for nations. History, then, is a record of an interruption of the course of nature. Soul-force, being natural, is not noted in history.

READER: According to what you say, it is plain that instances of the kind of passive resistance are not to be found in history. It is necessary to understand this passive resistance more fully. It will be better, therefore, if you enlarge upon it.

EDITOR: Passive resistance is a method of securing rights by personal suffering; it is the reverse of resistance by arms. When I refuse to do a thing that is repugnant to my conscience, I use soul-force. For instance, the government of the day has passed a law which is applicable to me: I do not like it, if, by using violence, I force the government to repeal the law, I am employing what may be termed body-force. If I do not obey the law and accept the penalty for its breach, I use soul-force. It involves sacrifice of self.

Everybody admits that sacrifice of self is infinitely superior to sacrifice of others. Moreover, if this kind of force is used in a cause that is unjust only the person using it suffers. He does not make others suffer for his mistakes. Men have before now done many things which were subsequently found to have been wrong. No man can claim to be absolutely in the right, or that a particular thing is wrong, because he thinks so, but it is wrong for him so long as that is his deliberate judgment. It is, therefore, meet that he should not do that which he knows to be wrong, and suffer the consequence whatever it may be. This is the key to the use of soul-force.

READER: You would then disregard laws—this is rank disloyalty. We have always been considered a law-abiding nation. You seem to be going even beyond the extremists. They say that we must obey the laws that have been passed, but that, if the laws be bad, we must drive out the law-givers even by force.

EDITOR: Whether I go beyond them or whether I do not, is a matter of no consequence to either of us. We simply want to find out what is right, and to act accordingly. The real meaning of the statement that we are a law-abiding nation is that we are passive resisters. When we do not like certain laws, we do not break the heads of law-givers, but we suffer and do not submit to the laws. That we should obey laws whether good or bad is a new-fangled notion. There was no such thing in former days. The people disregarded those laws they did not like, and suffered the penalties for their breach. It is contrary to our manhood, if we obey laws repugnant to our conscience. Such teaching is opposed to religion and means slavery. If the government were to ask us to go about without any clothing, should we do so? If I were a passive resister, I would say to them that I would have nothing to do with their law. But we have so forgotten ourselves and become so compliant, that we do not mind any degrading law.

A man who has realised his manhood, who fears only God, will fear no one else. Man-made laws are not necessarily binding on him. Even the government do not expect any such thing from us. They do not say: "You must do such and such a thing," but they say: "If you do not do it, we will punish you." We are sunk so low, that we fancy that it is our duty and our religion to do what the law lays down. If man will only realise that it is unmanly to obey laws that are unjust, no man's tyranny will enslave him. This is the key to self-rule or home-rule.

It is a superstition and an ungodly thing to believe that an act of a majority binds a minority. Many examples can be given in which acts of majorities will be found to have been wrong, and those of minorities to have been right. All reforms owe their origin to the initiation of minorities in opposition to majorities. If among a band of robbers, a knowledge of robbing is obligatory, is a pious man to accept the obligation? So long as the superstition that men should obey unjust laws exists, so long will their slavery exist. And a passive resister alone can remove such a superstition.

To use brute-force, to use gun-powder is contrary to passive resistance; for it means that we want our opponent to do by force—that which we desire but he does not. And, if such a use of force is justifiable, surely he is entitled to do likewise by us. And so we should never come to an agreement. We may simply fancy, like the blind horse moving in a circle round a mill, that we are making progress. Those who believe that they are not bound to obey laws which are repugnant to their conscience have only the remedy of passive resistance open to them. Any other must lead to disaster.

READER: From what you say, I deduce that passive resistance is a splendid weapon of the weak but that, when they are strong, they may take up arms.

EDITOR: This is gross ignorance. Passive resistance, that is, soul-force, is matchless. It is superior to the force of arms. How, then, can it be considered only a weapon of the weak? Physical force men are strangers to the courage that is requisite in a passive resister. Do you believe that a coward can ever disobey a law that he dislikes? Extremists are considered to be advocates of brute-force. Why do they, then, talk about obeying laws? I do not blame them. They can say nothing else. When they succeed in driving out the English, and they themselves become governors, they will want you and me to obey their laws. And that is a fitting thing for their constitution. But a passive resister will say he will not obey a law that is against his conscience, even though he may be blown to pieces at the mouth of a cannon.

What do you think? Wherein is courage required—in blowing others to pieces from behind a cannon or with a smiling face to approach a cannon and to be blown to pieces? Who is the true warrior—he who keeps death always as a bosom-friend or he who controls the death of others? Believe me that a man devoid of courage and manhood can never be a passive resister.

This, however, I will admit: that even a man, weak in body, is capable of offering this resistance. One man can offer it just as well as millions. Both men and women can indulge in it. It does not require the training of an army; it needs no Jiu-jitsu. Control over the mind is alone necessary, and, when that is attained, man is free like the king of the forest, and his very glance withers the enemy.

Passive resistance is an all-sided sword; it can be used anyhow; it blesses him who uses it and him against whom it is used. Without drawing a drop of blood, it produces far-reaching results. It never rusts, and cannot be stolen. Competition between passive resisters does not exhaust. The sword of passive resistance does not require a scabbard. It is strange indeed that you should consider such a weapon to be a weapon merely of the weak.

READER: You have said that passive resistance is a speciality of India. Have cannons never been used in India?

EDITOR: Evidently, in your opinion, India means its few princes. To me, it means its teeming millions, on whom depends the existence of its princes and our own.

Kings will always use their kingly weapons. To use force is bred in them. They want to command, but those who have to obey commands, do not want guns; and these are in a majority throughout the world. They have to learn either body-force or soul-force. Where they learn the former, both the rulers and the ruled become like so many mad men, but, where they learn soul-force, the commands of the rulers do not go beyond the point of their swords, for true men disregard unjust commands. Peasants have never been subdued by the sword, and never will be. They do not know the use of the sword, and they are not frightened by the use of it by others. That nation is great which rests its head upon death as its pillow. Those who defy death are free from all fear. For those who are labouring under the delusive charms of brute-force, this picture is not overdrawn. The fact is that, in India, the nation at large has generally used passive resistance in all departments of life. We cease to co-operate with our rulers when they displease us. This is passive resistance.

I remember an instance when, in a small principality, the villagers were offended by some command issued by the prince. The former immediately began vacating the village. The prince became nervous, apologised to his subjects and withdrew his command. Many such instances can be found in India. Real home-rule is possible only where passive resistance is the guiding force of the people. Any other rule is foreign rule.

READER: Then you will say that it is not at all necessary for us to train the body?

EDITOR: I will certainly not say any such thing. It is difficult to become a passive resister, unless the body is trained. As a rule, the mind, residing in a body that has become weakened by pampering, is also weak, and where there is no strength of mind, there can be no strength of soul. We will have to improve our physique by getting rid of infant marriages and luxurious living. If I were to ask a man having a shattered body to face a cannon's mouth I would make of myself a laughing-stock.

READER: From what you say, then, it would appear that it is not a small thing to become a passive resister, and, if that is so, I would like you to explain how a man may become a passive resister.

EDITOR: To become a passive resister is easy enough, but it is also equally difficult. I have known a lad of fourteen years become a passive resister; I have known also sick people doing likewise and I have also known physically strong and otherwise happy people being unable to take up passive resistance. After a great deal of experience, it seems to me that those who want to become passive resisters for the service of the country have to observe perfect chastity, adopt poverty, follow truth, and cultivate fearlessness.

Chastity is one of the greatest disciplines without which the mind cannot attain requisite firmness. A man who is unchaste loses stamina, becomes emasculated and cowardly. He whose mind is given over to animal passions is not capable of any great effort. This can be proved by innumerable instances. What, then, is a married person to do, is the question that arises naturally; and yet it need not. When a husband and wife gratify the passions, it is no less an animal indulgence on that account. Such an indulgence, except for perpetuating the race, is strictly prohibited. But a passive resister has to avoid even that very limited indulgence, because he can have no desire for progeny. A married man, therefore, can observe perfect chastity. This subject is not capable of being treated at greater length. Several questions arise: How is one to carry one's wife with one? What are her rights, and such other questions? Yet those who wish to take part in a great work are bound to solve these puzzles.

Just as there is necessity for chastity, so is there for poverty. Pecuniary ambition and passive resistance cannot well go together. Those who have money are not expected to throw it away, but they are expected to be indifferent about it. They must be prepared to lose every penny rather than give up passive resistance.

Passive resistance has been described in the course of our discussion as truth-force. Truth, therefore, has necessarily to be followed, and that at any cost. In this connection, academic questions such as whether a man may not lie in order to save a life, etc. arise, but these questions occur only to those who wish to justify lying. Those who want to follow truth every time are not placed in such a quandary, and, if they are, they are still saved from a false position.

Passive resistance cannot proceed a step without fearlessness. Those alone can follow the path of passive resistance who are free from fear whether as to their possessions, false honour, their relatives, the government, bodily injuries, death.

These observances are not to be abandoned in the belief that they are difficult. Nature has implanted in the human breast ability to cope with any difficulty or suffering that may come to man unprovoked. These qualities are worth having, even for those who do not wish to serve the country. Let there be no mistake as those who want to train themselves in the use of arms are also obliged to have these qualities more or less. Everybody does not become a warrior for the wish. A would-be warrior will have to observe chastity, and to be satisfied with poverty as his lot. A warrior without fearlessness cannot be conceived of. It may be thought that he would not need to be exactly truthful, but that quality follows real fearlessness. When a man abandons truth, he does so owing to fear in some shape or form. The above four attributes, then, need not frighten any one. It may be as well here to note that a physical-force man has to have many other useless qualities which a passive resister never needs. And you will find that whatever extra effort a swordsman needs is due to lack of fearlessness. If he is an embodiment of the latter, the sword will drop from his hand that very moment. He does not need its support. One who is free from hatred requires no sword. A man with a stick suddenly came face to face with a lion, and instinctively raised his weapon in self-defence. The man saw that he had only prated about fearlessness when there was none in him. That moment he dropped the stick, and found himself free from all fear.

Chapter XVIII
Education

R EADER: In the whole of our discussion, you have not demonstrated the necessity for education; we always complain of its absence among us. We notice a movement for compulsory education in our country. The Maharaja of Gaekwar has introduced it in his territories. Every eye is directed towards them. We bless the Maharaja for it. Is all this effort then of no use?

EDITOR: If we consider our civilization to be the highest, I have regretfully to say that much of the effort you have described is of no use. The motive of the Maharaja and other great leaders who have been working in this direction is perfectly pure. They, therefore, undoubtedly deserve great praise. But we cannot conceal from ourselves the result that is likely to flow from their effort.

What is the meaning of education? If it simply means a knowledge of letters, it is merely an instrument, and an instrument may be well used or abused. The same instrument that may be used to cure a patient may be used to take his life, and so may a knowledge of letters. We daily observe that many men abuse it, and very few make good use of it, and if this is a correct statement, we have proved that more harm has been done by it than good.

The ordinary meaning of education is a knowledge of letters. To teach boys reading, writing and arithmetic is called primary education. A peasant earns his bread honestly. He has ordinary knowledge of the world. He knows fairly well how he should behave towards his parents, his wife, his children and his fellow-villagers. He understands and observes the rules of morality. But he cannot write his own name. What do you propose to do by giving him a knowledge of letters? Will you add an inch to his happiness? Do you wish to make him discontented with his cottage or his lot? And even if you want to do that, he will not need such an education. Carried away by the flood of western thought, we came to the conclusion, without weighing *pros* and *cons*, that we should give this kind of education to the people.

Now let us take higher education. I have learned Geography, Astronomy, Algebra, Geometry, etc. What of that? In what way have I benefitted myself or those around me? Why have I learned these things? Professor Huxley has thus defined education:—"That man I think has had a liberal education who has been so trained in youth that his body is the ready servant of his will and does with ease and pleasure all the work that as a mechanism it is capable of, whose intellect is a clear, cold logic engine with all its parts of equal strength and in smooth working order ... whose mind is stored with a knowledge of the fundamental truths of nature ... whose passions are trained to come to heel by a vigorous will, the servant of a tender conscience ... who has learnt to hate all vileness and to respect others as himself. Such an one and no other, I conceive, has had a liberal education, for he is in harmony with Nature. He will make the best of her and she of him."

If this be true education, I must emphatically say that the sciences I have enumerated above, I have never been able to use for controlling my senses. Therefore, whether you take elementary education or higher education, it is not required for the main thing. It does not make of us men. It does not enable us to do our duty.

READER: If that is so, I shall have to ask you another question. What enables you to tell all these things to me? If you had not received higher education, how would you have been able to explain to me the things that you have?

EDITOR: You have spoken well. But my answer is simple: I do not for one moment believe that my life would have been wasted, had I not received higher or lower education. Nor do I consider that I necessarily serve because I speak. But I do desire to serve and, in endeavouring to fulfil that desire, I make use of the education I have received. And, if I am making good use of it, even then it is not for the millions, but I can use it only for such as you, and this supports my contention. Both you and I have come under the bane of what is mainly false education. I claim to have become free from its ill-effects, and I am trying to give you the benefit of my experience, and, in doing so, I am demonstrating the rottenness of this education.

Moreover, I have not run down a knowledge of letters under all circumstances. All I have shown is that we must not make of it a fetish. It is not our Kamdhuk. In its place it can be of use, and it has its place when we have brought our senses under subjection, and put our ethics on a firm foundation. And then, if we feel inclined to receive that education, we may make good use of it. As an ornament it is likely to sit well on us. It now follows that it is not necessary to make this education compulsory. Our ancient school system is enough. Character-building has the first place in it, and that is primary education. A building erected on that foundation will last.

READER: Do I then understand that you do not consider English education necessary for obtaining Home Rule?

EDITOR: My answer is yes and no. To give millions a knowledge of English is to enslave them. The foundation that Macaulay laid of education has enslaved us. I do not suggest that he had any such intention, but that has been the result. Is it not a sad commentary that we should have to speak of Home Rule in a foreign tongue?

And it is worthy of note that the systems which the Europeans have discarded are the systems in vogue among us. Their learned men continually make changes. We ignorantly adhere to their cast-off systems. They are trying each division to improve its own status. Wales is a small portion of England. Great efforts are being made to revive a knowledge of Welsh among Welshmen. The English Chancellor, Mr. Lloyd George, is taking a leading part in the movement to make Welsh children speak Welsh. And what is our condition? We write to each other in faulty English, and from this even, our M. A.'s are not free; our best thoughts are expressed in English; the proceedings of our Congress are conducted in English; our best newspapers are printed in English. If this state of things continues for a long time, posterity will—it is my firm opinion— condemn and curse us.

It is worth noting that, by receiving English education, we have enslaved the nation. Hypocrisy, tyranny, etc., have increased; English-knowing Indians have not hesitated to cheat and strike terror into the people. Now, if we are doing anything for the people at all, we are paying only a portion of the debt due to them.

Is it not a most painful thing that, if I want to go to a court of justice, I must employ the English language as medium; that, when I become a barrister, I may not speak my mother-tongue, and that some one else should have to translate to me from my own language? Is not this absolutely absurd? Is it not a sign of slavery? Am I to blame the English for it or myself? It is we, the English-knowing men, that have enslaved India. The curse of the nation will rest not upon the English but upon us.

I have told you that my answer to your last question is both yes and no. I have explained to you why it is yes. I shall now explain why it is no.

We are so much beset by the disease of civilization, that we cannot altogether do without English education. Those who have already received it may make good use of it wherever necessary. In our dealings with the English people, in our dealings with our own people, when we can only correspond with them through that language, and for the purpose of knowing how much disgusted they (the English) have themselves become with their civilization, we may use or learn English, as the case may be. Those who have studied English will have to teach morality to their progeny through their mother-tongue, and to teach them another Indian language; but when they have grown up, they may learn English, the ultimate aim being that we should not need it. The object of making money thereby should be eschewed. Even in learning English to such a limited extent we will have to consider what we should learn through it and what we should not. It will be necessary to know what sciences we should learn. A little thought should show you that immediately we cease to care for English degrees, the rulers will prick up their ears.

READER: Then what education shall we give?

waste our money, but by reproducing Manchester in India, we shall keep our money at the price of our blood, because our very moral being will be sapped, and I call in support of my statement the very mill-hands as witnesses. And those who have amassed wealth out of factories are not likely to be better than other rich men. It would be folly to assume that an Indian Rockfeller would be better than the American Rockfeller. Impoverished India can become free, but it will be hard for an India, made rich through immorality, to regain its freedom. I fear we will have to admit that moneyed men support British rule; their interest is bound up with its stability. Money renders a man helpless. The other thing is as harmful as sexual vice. Both are poison. A snakebite is a lesser poison than these two, because the former merely destroys the body, but the latter destroys body, mind and soul. We need not, therefore, be pleased with the prospect of the growth of the mill-industry.

READER: Are the mills, then, to be closed down?

EDITOR: That is difficult. It is no easy task to do away with a thing that is established. We, therefore, say that the non-beginning of a thing is, supreme wisdom. We cannot condemn mill-owners, we can but pity them. It would be too much to expect them to give up their mills, but we may implore them not to increase them. If they would be good, they would gradually contract their business. They can establish in thousands of households the ancient and sacred handlooms, and they can buy out the cloth that may be thus woven. Whether the mill-owners do this or not, people can cease to use machine-made goods.

READER: You have so far spoken about machine-made cloth, but there are innumerable machine-made things. We have either to import them or to introduce machinery into our country.

EDITOR: Indeed, our gods even are made in Germany. What need, then, to speak of matches, pins, and glassware? My answer can be only one. What did India do before these articles were introduced? Precisely the same should be done to-day. As long as we cannot make pins without machinery, so long will we do without them. The tinsel splendour of glassware we will have nothing to do with and we will make wicks, as of old, with home-grown cotton, and use hand-made earthern saucers for lamps. So doing, we shall save our eyes and money, and will support Swadeshi, and so shall we attain Home Rule.

It is not to be conceived that all men will do all these things at one time, or that some men will give up all machine-made things at once. But, if the thought is sound, we will always find out what we can give up, and will gradually cease to use this. What a few may do, others will copy, and the movement will grow like the cocoanut of the mathematical problem. What the leaders do, the populace will gladly follow. The matter is neither complicated nor difficult. You and I shall not wait until we can carry others with us. Those will be the losers who will not do it, and those who will not do it, although they can appreciate the truth, will deserve to be called cowards.

READER: What, then, of the tram-cars and electricity?

EDITOR: This question is now too late. It signifies nothing. If we are to do without the railways, we shall have to do without the tram-cars. Machinery is like a snake-hole which may contain from one to a hundred snakes. Where there is machinery there are large cities; and where there are large cities, there are tram-cars and railways; and there only does one see electric light. English villages do not boast any of these things. Honest physicians will tell you that, where means of artificial locomotion have increased, the health of the people has suffered. I remember that, when in a European town there was a scarcity of money, the receipts of the tramway company, of the lawyers and of the doctors, went down, and the people were less unhealthy. I cannot recall a single good point in connection with machinery. Books can be written to demonstrate its evils.

READER: It is a good point or a bad one that all you are saying will be printed through machinery?

EDITOR: This is one of those instances which demonstrate that sometimes poison is used to kill poison. This, then, will not be a good point regarding machinery. As it expires, the machinery, as it were, says to us: "Beware and avoid me. You will derive no benefit from me, and the benefit that may accrue from printing will avail only those who are infected with the machinery-craze." Do not, therefore, forget the main thing. It is necessary to realise that machinery is bad. We shall then be able gradually to do away with it. Nature has not provided any way whereby we may reach a desired goal all of a sudden. If, instead of welcoming machinery as a boon, we would look upon it as an evil, it would ultimately go.

Chapter XX
Conclusion

READER: From your views I gather that you would form a third party. You are neither an extremist nor a moderate.

EDITOR: That is a mistake. I do not think of a third party at all. We do not all think alike. We cannot say that all the moderates hold identical views. And how can those who want to serve only have a party? I would serve both the moderates and the extremists. Where I should differ from them, I would respectfully place my position before them, and continue my service.

READER: What, then, would you say to both the parties?

EDITOR: I would say to the extremists:—"I know that you want Home Rule for India; it is not to be had for your asking. Everyone will have to take it for himself. What others get for me is not Home Rule but foreign rule; therefore, it would not be proper for you to say that you have obtained Home Rule, if you expelled the English. I have already described the true nature of Home Rule. This you would never obtain by force of arms. Brute-force is not natural to the Indian soil. You will have, therefore, to rely wholly on soul-force. You must not consider that violence is necessary at any stage for reaching our goal."

I would say to the moderates:—"Mere petitioning is derogatory; we thereby confess inferiority. To say that British rule is indispensable, is almost a denial of the Godhead. We cannot say that anybody or anything is indispensable except God. Moreover, commonsense should tell us that to state that, for the time being, the presence of the English in India is a necessity, is to make them conceited.

"If the English vacated India bag and baggage, it must not be supposed that she would be widowed. It is possible that those who are forced to observe peace under their pressure would fight after their withdrawal. There can be no advantage in suppressing an eruption, it must have its vent. If, therefore, before we can remain at peace, we must fight amongst ourselves, it is better that we do so. There is no occasion for a third party to protect the weak. It is this so-called protection which has unnerved us. Such protection can only make the weak weaker. Unless we realise this, we cannot have Home Rule. I would paraphrase the thought of an English divine and say that anarchy under home rule were better than orderly foreign rule. Only, the meaning that the learned divine attached to home rule is different to Indian Home Rule according to my conception. We have to learn, and to teach others, that we do not want the tyranny of their English rule or Indian rule."

If this idea were carried out both the extremists and the moderates could join hands. There is no occasion to fear or distrust one another.

READER: What, then, would you say to the English?

EDITOR: To them I would respectfully say: "I admit you are my rulers. It is not necessary to debate the question whether you hold India by the sword or by my consent. I have no objection to your remaining in my country, but although you are the rulers, you will have to remain as servants of the people. It is not we who have to do as you wish, but it is you who have to do as we wish. You may keep the riches that you have drained away from this land, but you may not drain riches henceforth. Your function will be, if you so wish, to police India; you must abandon the idea of deriving any commercial benefit from us. We hold the civilization that you support to be the reverse of civilization. We consider our civilization to be far superior to yours. If you realise this truth, it will be to your advantage, and, if you do not, according to your own proverb, you should only live in our country in the same manner as we do. You must not do anything that is contrary to our religions. It is your duty as rulers that, for the sake of the Hindus, you should eschew beef, and for the sake of the Mahomedans, you should avoid bacon and ham. We have hitherto said nothing, because we have been cowed down, but you need not consider that you have not hurt our feelings by your conduct. We are not expressing our sentiments either through base selfishness or fear, but because it is our duty now to speak out boldly. We consider your schools and law courts to be useless. We want our own ancient schools and courts to be restored. The common language of India is not English but Hindi. You should, therefore, learn it. We can hold communication with you only in our national language.

"We cannot tolerate the idea of your spending money on railways and the military. We see no occasion for either. You may fear Russia; we do not. When she comes we will look after her. If you are with us, we will then receive her jointly. We do not need any European cloth. We will manage with articles produced and manufactured at home. You may not keep one eye on Manchester and the other on India. We can work together only if our interests are identical.

"This has not been said to you in arrogance. You have great military resources. Your naval power is matchless. If we wanted to fight with you on your own ground we would be unable to do so, but, if the above submissions be not acceptable to you, we cease to play the ruled. You may, if you like, cut us to pieces. You may shatter us at the cannon's mouth. If you act contrary to our will, we will not help you and, without our help, we know that you cannot move one step forward.

"It is likely that you will laugh at all this in the intoxication of your power. We may not be able to disillusion you at once, but, if there be any manliness in us, you will see shortly that your intoxication is suicidal, and that your laugh at our expense is an aberration of intellect. We believe that, at heart you belong to a religious nation. We are living in a land which is the source of religions. How we came together need not be considered, but we can make mutual good use of our relations.

"You English who have come to India are not a good specimen of the English nation, nor can we almost half Anglicised Indians, be considered a good specimen of the real Indian nation. If the English nation were to know all you have done, it would oppose many of your actions. The mass of the Indians have had few dealings with you. If you will abandon your so-called civilization, and search into your own scriptures, you will find that our demands are just. Only on conditions of our demands being fully satisfied may you remain in India, and, if you remain under those conditions we shall learn several things from you, and you will learn many from us. So doing, we shall benefit each other and the world. But that will happen only when the root of our relationship is sunk in a religious soil."

READER: What will you say to the nation?

EDITOR: Who is the nation?

READER: For our purposes it is the nation that you and I have been thinking of, that is, those of us who are affected by European civilization, and who are eager to have Home Rule.

EDITOR: To these I would say: It is only those Indians who are imbued with real love who will be able to speak to the English in the above strain without being frightened, and those only can be said to be so imbued who conscientiously believe that Indian civilization is the best, and that European is a nine days' wonder. Such ephemeral civilizations have often come and gone, and will continue to do so. Those only can be considered to be so imbued, who, having experienced the force of the soul within themselves, will not cower before brute-force, and will not, on any account, desire to use brute-force. Those only can be considered to have been so imbued who are intensely dissatisfied with the present pitiable condition having already drunk the cup of poison.

If there be only one such Indian, he will speak as above to the English, and the English will have to listen to him.

These demands are not demands, but they show our mental state. We will get nothing by asking; we shall have to take what we want, and we need the requisite strength for the effort and that strength will be available to him only who

1. will, only on rare occasions, make use of the English language;
2. if a lawyer, will give up his profession and take up a hand-loom;
3. if a lawyer, will devote his knowledge to enlightening both his people and the English;
4. if a lawyer, will not meddle with the quarrels between parties, but will give up the courts and from his experience induce the people to do

likewise;

5. if a lawyer, will refuse to be a judge, as he will give up his profession;

6. if a doctor, will give up medicine, and understand that rather than mending bodies, he should mend souls;

7. if a doctor, will understand, that no matter to what religion he belongs, it is better that bodies remain diseased rather than that they are cured through the instrumentality of the diabolical vivisection that is practised in European schools of medicine;

8. although a doctor, will take up a hand-loom and, if any patients come to him, will tell them the cause of their diseases, and will advise them to remove the cause, rather than pamper them by giving useless drugs; he will understand that, if by not taking drugs, perchance the patient dies, the world will not come to grief, and that he will have been really merciful to him;

9. although a wealthy man, regardless of his wealth, will speak out his mind and fear no one;

10. if a wealthy man, will devote his money to establishing hand-looms, and encourage others to use hand-made goods by wearing them himself;

11. like every other Indian, will know that this is a time for repentance, expiation and mourning;

12. like every other Indian, will know that to blame the English is useless, that they came because of us, and remain also for the same reason, and that they will either go or change their nature, only when we reform ourselves;

13. like others, will understand that, at a time of mourning, there can be no indulgence, and that, whilst we are in a fallen state, to be in gaol or in banishment is much the best;

14. like others, will know that it is superstition to imagine it necessary that we should guard against being imprisoned in order that we may deal with the people;

15. like others, will know that action is much better than speech; that it is our duty to say exactly what we think and face the consequences, and that it will be only then that we shall be able to impress anybody with our speech;

16. like others, will understand that we will become free only through suffering;
17. like others, will understand that deportation for life to the Andamans is not enough expiation for the sin of encouraging European civilization;
18. like others, will know that no nation has risen without suffering; that, even in physical warfare, the true test is suffering and not the killing of others, much more so in the warfare of passive resistance;
19. like others, will know that it is an idle excuse to say that we will do a thing when the others also do it; that we should do what we know to be right, and that others will do it when they see the way; that when I fancy a particular delicacy, I do not wait till others taste it; that to make a national effort and to suffer are in the nature of delicacies; and that to suffer under pressure is no suffering.

READER: This is a large order. When will all carry it out?

EDITOR: You make a mistake. You and I have nothing to do with the others. Let each do his duty. If I do my duty, that is, serve myself, I shall be able to serve others. Before I leave you, I will take the liberty of repeating.
1. Real home-rule is self-rule or self-control.
2. The way to it is passive resistance: that is soul force or love-force.
3. In order to exert this force, Swadeshi in every sense is necessary.
4. What we want to do should be done, not because we object to the English or that we want to retaliate, but because it is our duty to do so. Thus, supposing that the English remove the salt-tax, restore our money, give the highest posts to Indians, withdraw the English troops, we shall certainly not use their machine-made goods, nor use the English language, nor many of their industries. It is worth noting that these things are, in their nature, harmful; hence, we do not want them. I bear no enmity towards the English, but I do towards their civilization.

In my opinion, we have used the term "Swaraj" without understanding its real significance. I have endeavoured to explain it as I understand it, and my conscience testifies that my life henceforth is dedicated to its attainment.

APPENDICES:

SOME AUTHORITIES
TESTIMONIES BY EMINENT MEN

APPENDICES

SOME AUTHORITIES

The following books are recommended for perusal to follow up the study of the foregoing:—

"The Kingdom of God is Within You"—*Tolstoy.*
"What is Art?"—*Tolstoy.*
"Slavery of Our Times"—*Tolstoy.*
"The First Step"—*Tolstoy.*
"How Shall We Escape"—*Tolstoy.*
"Letter to a Hindoo"—*Tolstoy.*
"The White Slaves of England"—*Sherard.*
"Civilization: Its Cause and Cure"—*Carpenter.*
"The Fallacy of Speed"—*Taylor.*
"A New Crusade"—*Blount.*
"On the Duty of Civil Disobedience"—*Thoreau.*
"Life Without Principle"—*Thoreau.*
"Unto This Last"—*Ruskin.*
"A Joy for Ever"—*Ruskin.*
"Duties of Man"—*Mazzini.*
"Defence and Death of Socrates"—From *Plato.*
"Paradoxes of Civilization"—*Max Nordau.*
"Poverty and Un-British Rule in India"—*Naoroji.*
"Economic History of India"—*Dutt.*
"Village Communities"—*Maine.*

TESTIMONIES BY EMINENT MEN

The following extracts from Mr. Alfred Webb's valuable collection, if the testimony given therein be true, show that the ancient Indian civilization, has little to learn from the modern:—

VICTOR COUSIN
(1792—1867). Founder of Systematic Eclecticism in Philosophy.

"On the other hand when we read with attention the poetical and philosophical movements of the East, above all, those of India, which are beginning to spread in Europe, we discover there so many truths, and truths so profound, and which make such a contrast with the meanness of the results at which the European genius has sometimes stopped, that we are constrained to bend the knee before that of the East, and to see in this cradle of the human race the native land of the highest philosophy."

J. SEYMOUR KEAY, M. P.
Banker in India and India Agent.
(Writing in 1883.)

"It cannot be too well understood that our position in India has never been in any degree that of civilians bringing civilization to savage races. When we landed in India we found there a hoary civilization, which, during the progress of thousands of years, had fitted itself into the character and adjusted itself to the wants of highly intellectual races. The civilization was not prefunctory, but universal and all-pervading— furnishing the country not only with political systems but with social and domestic institutions of the most ramified description. The beneficent nature of these institutions as a whole may be judged of from their effects on the character of the Hindu race. Perhaps there are no other people in the world who show so much in their characters the advantageous effects of their own civilization. They are shrewd in business, acute in reasoning, thrifty, religious, sober, charitable, obedient to parents, reverential to old age, amiable, law-abiding, compassionate towards the helpless, and patient under suffering."

FRIEDRICH MAX MUELIER, LL.D.

"If I were to ask myself from what literature we hear in Europe, we who have been nurtured almost exclusively on the thoughts of Greeks and Romans, and of one Semetic race, the Jewish may draw that corrective which is most wanted in order to make our inner life more perfect, more comprehensive, more universal, in fact more truly human, a life, not for this life only but a transfigured and eternal life—again I should point to India."

MICHAEL G. MULHALL, F.R.S.S.

Statistics (1899).

Prison population per 100,000 of inhabitants:

Several European States	100 to 230
England and Wales	90
India	38

—*"Dictionary of Statistics," Michael G. Mulhall, F.R.S.S., Routledge and Sons, 1899.*

COLONEL THOMAS MUNRO
Thirty-two years' service in India.

"If a good system of agriculture, unrivalled manufacturing skill, a capacity to produce whatever can contribute to convenience or luxury; schools established in every village, for teaching, reading, writing and arithmetic; the general practice of hospitality and charity among each other; and, above all, treatment of the female sex, full of confidence, respect and delicacy, are among the signs which denote a civilised people, then the Hindus are not inferior to the nations of Europe; and if civilization is to become an article of trade between the two countries, I am convinced that this country [England] will gain by the import cargo."

Frederick von Schlegel

"It cannot be denied that the early Indians possessed a knowledge of the true God; all their writings are replete with sentiments and expressions noble, clear and severely grand, as deeply conceived and reverently expressed as in any human language in which men have spoken of their God.... Among nations possessing indigenous philosophy and metaphysics, together with an innate relish for these pursuits, such as at present characterises Germany; and in olden times, was the proud distinction of Greece, Hindustan holds the first rank in point of time."

Sir William Wedderburn, Bart

"The Indian village has thus for centuries remained a bulwark against political disorder, and the home of the simple domestic and social virtues. No wonder, therefore, that philosophers and historians have always dwelt lovingly on this ancient institution which is the natural social unit and the best type of rural life; self-contained, industrious, peace-loving, conservative in the best sense of the word.... I think you will agree with me that there is much that is both picturesque and attractive in this glimpse of social and domestic life in an Indian village. It is a harmless and happy form of human existence. Moreover, it is not without good practical outcome."

J. Young
Secretary, Savon Mechanics' Institutes.
(Within recent years).

"Those races, [the Indian viewed from a moral aspect] are perhaps the most remarkable people in the world. They breathe an atmosphere of moral purity, which cannot but excite admiration, and this is especially the case with the poorer classes who, notwithstanding the privations of their humble lot, appear to be happy and contented. True children of nature, they live on from day to day, taking no thought of to-morrow and thankful for the simple fare which Providence has provided for them. It is curious to witness the spectacle of coolies of both sexes returning home at nightfall after a hard day's work often lasting from sunrise to sunset. In spite of fatigue from the effects of the unremitting toil, they are, for the most part, gay and animated, conversing cheerfully together and occasionally breaking into snatches of light-hearted song. Yet what awaits them on their return to the hovels which they call home? A dish of rice for food, and the floor for a bed. Domestic felicity appears to be the rule among the Natives, and this is the more strange when the customs of marriage are taken into account, parents arranging all such matters. Many Indian households afford examples of the married state in its highest degree of perfection. This may be due to the teachings of the Shastras, and to the strict injunctions which they inculcate with regard to marital obligations; but it is no exaggeration to say that husbands are generally devotedly attached to their wives, and in many instances the latter have the most exalted conception of their duties towards their husbands."

ABBE J. A. DUBOIS
Missionary in Mysore. Extracts from letter dated Seringapatam,
15th December, 1820.

"The authority of married women within their houses is chiefly exerted in preserving good order and peace among the persons who compose their families: and a great many among them discharge this important duty with a prudence and a discretion which have scarcely a parallel in Europe. I have known families composed of between thirty and forty persons, or more, consisting of grown-up sons and daughters, all married and all having children, living together under the superintendence of an old matron—their mother or mother-in-law. The latter, by good management, and by accommodating herself to the temper of the daughters-in-law, by using, according to circumstances, firmness or forbearance, succeeded in preserving peace and harmony during many years amongst so many females, who had all jarring interests, and still more jarring tempers. I ask you whether it would be possible to attain the same end, in the same circumstances, in our countries, where it is scarcely possible to make two women living under the same foot to agree together.

"In fact, there is perhaps no kind of honest employment in a civilised country in which the Hindu females have not a due share. Besides the management of the household, and the care of the family, which (as already noticed) under their control, the wives and daughters of husbandmen attend and assist their husbands and fathers in the labours of agriculture. Those of tradesmen assist theirs in carrying on their trade. Merchants are attended and assisted by theirs in their shops. Many females are shopkeepers on their own account and without a knowledge of the alphabet or of the decimal scale, they keep by other means their accounts in excellent order, and are considered as still shrewder than the males themselves in their commercial dealings."

A Letter to a Hindu
The Subjection of India–
Its Cause and Cure

With an Introduction by
M. K. Gandhi

Leo Tolstoy

CONTENTS

INTRODUCTION

The letter printed below is a translation of Tolstoy's letter written in Russian in reply to one from the Editor of Free Hindustan. After having passed from hand to hand, this letter at last came into my possession through a friend who asked me, as one much interested in Tolstoy's writings, whether I thought it worth publishing. I at once replied in the affirmative, and told him I should translate it myself into Gujarati and induce others' to translate and publish it in various Indian vernaculars.

The letter as received by me was a type-written copy. It was therefore referred to the author, who confirmed it as his and kindly granted me permission to print it.

To me, as a humble follower of that great teacher whom I have long looked upon as one of my guides, it is a matter of honour to be connected with the publication of his letter, such especially as the one which is now being given to the world.

It is a mere statement of fact to say that every Indian, whether he owns up to it or not, has national aspirations. But there are as many opinions as there are Indian nationalists as to the exact meaning of that aspiration, and more especially as to the methods to be used to attain the end.

One of the accepted and 'time-honoured' methods to attain the end is that of violence. The assassination of Sir Curzon Wylie was an illustration of that method in its worst and most detestable form. Tolstoy's life has been devoted to replacing the method of violence for removing tyranny or securing reform by the method of non-resistance to evil. He would meet hatred expressed in violence by love expressed in self-suffering. He admits of no exception to whittle down this great and divine law of love. He applies it to all the problems that trouble mankind.

When a man like Tolstoy, one of the clearest thinkers in the western world, one of the greatest writers, one who as a soldier has known what violence is and what it can do, condemns Japan for having blindly followed the law of modern science, falsely so-called, and fears for that country 'the greatest calamities', it is for us to pause and consider whether, in our impatience of English rule, we do not want to replace one evil by another and a worse. India, which is the nursery of the great faiths of the world, will cease to be nationalist India, whatever else she may become, when she goes through the process of civilization in the shape of reproduction on that sacred soil of gun factories and the hateful industrialism which has reduced the people of Europe to a state of slavery, and all but stifled among them the best instincts which are the heritage of the human family.

If we do not want the English in India we must pay the price. Tolstoy indicates it. 'Do not resist evil, but also do not yourselves participate in evil—in the violent deeds of the administration of the law courts, the collection of taxes and, what is more important, of the soldiers, and no one in the world will enslave you', passionately declares the sage of Yasnaya Polyana. Who can question the truth of what he says in the following: 'A commercial company enslaved a nation comprising two hundred millions. Tell this to a man free from superstition and he will fail to grasp what these words mean. What does it mean that thirty thousand people, not athletes, but rather weak and ordinary people, have enslaved two hundred millions of vigorous, clever, capable, freedom-loving people? Do not the figures make it clear that not the English, but the Indians, have enslaved themselves?'

One need not accept all that Tolstoy says—some of his facts are not accurately stated—to realize the central truth of his indictment of the present system, which is to understand and act upon the irresistible power of the soul over the body, of love, which is an attribute of the soul, over the brute or body force generated by the stirring in us of evil passions.

There is no doubt that there is nothing new in what Tolstoy

preaches. But his presentation of the old truth is refreshingly forceful. His logic is unassailable. And above all he endeavours to practise what he preaches. He preaches to convince. He is sincere and in earnest. He commands attention.

[19th November, 1909]
M. K. Gandhi

A Letter to a Hindu

By Leo Tolstoy

All that exists is One. People only call this One by different names.
    The Vedas

God is love, and he that abideth in love abideth in God, and God abideth in him.
    I John iv. 16

God is one whole; we are the parts.
    Exposition of the Teaching of the Vedas by Vivekananda

I

D o not seek quiet and rest in those earthly realms where delusions and desires are engendered, for if thou dost, thou wilt be dragged through the rough wilderness of life, which is far from Me.

Whenever thou feelest that thy feet are becoming entangled in the interlaced roots of life, know that thou has strayed from the path to which I beckon thee: for I have placed thee in broad, smooth paths, which are strewn with flowers. I have put a light before thee, which thou canst follow and thus run without stumbling. KRISHNA.

I have received your letter and two numbers of your periodical, both of which interest me extremely. The oppression of a majority by a minority, and the demoralization inevitably resulting from it, is a phenomenon that has always occupied me and has done so most particularly of late. I will try to explain to you what I think about that subject in general, and particularly about the cause from which the dreadful evils of which you write in your letter, and in the Hindu periodical you have sent me, have arisen and continue to arise.

The reason for the astonishing fact that a majority of working people submit to a handful of idlers who control their labour and their very lives is always and everywhere the same—whether the oppressors and oppressed are of one race or whether, as in India and elsewhere, the oppressors are of a different nation.

This phenomenon seems particularly strange in India, for there more than two hundred million people, highly gifted both physically and mentally, find themselves in the power of a small group of people quite alien to them in thought, and immeasurably inferior to them in religious morality.

From your letter and the articles in *Free Hindustan* as well as from the very interesting writings of the Hindu Swami Vivekananda and others, it appears that, as is the case in our time with the ills of all nations, the reason lies in the lack of a reasonable religious teaching which by explaining the meaning of life would supply a supreme law for the guidance of conduct and would replace the more than dubious precepts of pseudo-religion and pseudo-science with the immoral conclusions deduced from them and commonly called 'civilization'.

Your letter, as well as the articles in *Free Hindustan* and Indian political literature generally, shows that most of the leaders of public opinion among your people no longer attach any significance to the religious teachings that were and are professed by the peoples of India, and recognize no possibility of freeing the people from the oppression they endure except by adopting the irreligious and profoundly immoral social arrangements under which the English and other pseudo-Christian nations live to-day.

And yet the chief if not the sole cause of the enslavement of the Indian peoples by the English lies in this very absence of a religious consciousness and of the guidance for conduct which should flow from it—a lack common in our day to all nations East and West, from Japan to England and America alike.

II

_____

O ye, who see perplexities over your heads, beneath your feet, and to the right and left of you; you will be an eternal enigma unto yourselves until ye become humble and joyful as children. Then will ye find Me, and having found Me in yourselves, you will rule over worlds, and looking out from the great world within to the little world without, you will bless everything that is, and find all is well with time and with you.
KRISHNA.

T o make my thoughts clear to you I must go farther back. We do not, cannot, and I venture to say need not, know how men lived millions of years ago or even ten thousand years ago, but we do know positively that, as far back as we have any knowledge of mankind, it has always lived in special groups of families, tribes, and nations in which the majority, in the conviction that it must be so, submissively and willingly bowed to the rule of one or more persons—that is to a very small minority. Despite all varieties of circumstances and personalities these relations manifested themselves among the various peoples of whose origin we have any knowledge; and the farther back we go the more absolutely necessary did this arrangement appear, both to the rulers and the ruled, to make it possible for people to live peacefully together.

So it was everywhere. But though this external form of life existed for centuries and still exists, very early—thousands of years before our time—amid this life based on coercion, one and the same thought constantly emerged among different nations, namely, that in every individual a spiritual element is manifested that gives life to all that exists, and that this spiritual element strives to unite with everything of a like nature to itself, and attains this aim through love. This thought appeared in most various forms at different times and places, with varying completeness and clarity. It found expression in Brahmanism, Judaism, Mazdaism (the teachings of Zoroaster), in Buddhism, Taoism, Confucianism, and in the writings of the Greek and Roman sages, as well as in Christianity and Mohammedanism. The mere fact that this thought has sprung up among different nations and at different times indicates that it is inherent in human nature and contains the truth. But this truth was made known to people who considered that a community could only be kept together if some of them restrained others, and so it appeared quite irreconcilable with the existing order of society. Moreover it was at first expressed only fragmentarily, and so obscurely that though people admitted its theoretic truth they could not entirely accept it as guidance for their conduct. Then, too, the dissemination of the truth in a society based on coercion was always hindered in one and the same manner, namely, those in power, feeling that the recognition of this truth would undermine their position, consciously or sometimes unconsciously perverted it by explanations and additions quite foreign to it, and also opposed it by open violence. Thus the truth—that his life should be directed by the spiritual element which is its basis, which manifests itself as love, and which is so natural to man—this truth, in order to force a way to man's consciousness, had to struggle not merely against the obscurity with which it was expressed and the intentional and unintentional distortions surrounding it, but also against deliberate violence, which by means of persecutions and punishments sought to compel men to accept religious laws authorized by the rulers and conflicting with the truth. Such a hindrance and misrepresentation of the truth—which had not yet achieved complete clarity—occurred everywhere: in Confucianism and Taoism, in Buddhism and in Christianity, in Mohammedanism and in your Brahmanism.

III

My hand has sowed love everywhere, giving unto all that will receive. Blessings are offered unto all My children, but many times in their blindness they fail to see them. How few there are who gather the gifts which lie in profusion at their feet: how many there are, who, in wilful waywardness, turn their eyes away from them and complain with a wail that they have not that which I have given them; many of them defiantly repudiate not only My gifts, but Me also, Me, the Source of all blessings and the Author of their being. KRISHNA.

I tarry awhile from the turmoil and strife of the world. I will beautify and quicken thy life with love and with joy, for the light of the soul is Love. Where Love is, there is contentment and peace, and where there is contentment and peace, there am I, also, in their midst. KRISHNA.

The aim of the sinless One consists in acting without causing sorrow to others, although he could attain to great power by ignoring their feelings.

The aim of the sinless One lies in not doing evil unto those who have done evil unto him.

If a man causes suffering even to those who hate him without any reason, he will ultimately have grief not to be overcome.

The punishment of evil doers consists in making them feel ashamed of themselves by doing them a great kindness.

Of what use is superior knowledge in the one, if he does not endeavour to relieve his neighbour's want as much as his own?

If, in the morning, a man wishes to do evil unto another, in the evening the evil will return to him.

THE HINDU KURAL

Thus it went on everywhere. The recognition that love represents the highest morality was nowhere denied or contradicted, but this truth was so interwoven everywhere with all kinds of falsehoods which distorted it, that finally nothing of it remained but words. It was taught that this highest morality was only applicable to private life—for home use, as it were—but that in public life all forms of violence—such as imprisonment, executions, and wars—might be used for the protection of the majority against a minority of evildoers, though such means were diametrically opposed to any vestige of love. And though common sense indicated that if some men claim to decide who is to be subjected to violence of all kinds for the benefit of others, these men to whom violence is applied may, in turn, arrive at a similar conclusion with regard to those who have employed violence to them, and though the great religious teachers of Brahmanism, Buddhism, and above all of Christianity, foreseeing such a perversion of the law of love, have constantly drawn attention to the one invariable condition of love (namely, the enduring of injuries, insults, and violence of all kinds without resisting evil by evil) people continued—regardless of all that leads man forward—to try to unite the incompatibles: the virtue of love, and what is opposed to love, namely, the restraining of evil by violence. And such a teaching, despite its inner contradiction, was so firmly established that the very people who recognize love as a virtue accept as lawful at the same time an order of life based on violence and allowing men not merely to torture but even to kill one another.

For a long time people lived in this obvious contradiction without noticing it. But a time arrived when this contradiction became more and more evident to thinkers of various nations. And the old and simple truth that it is natural for men to help and to love one another, but not to torture and to kill one another, became ever clearer, so that fewer and fewer people were able to believe the sophistries by which the distortion of the truth had been made so plausible.

In former times the chief method of justifying the use of violence and thereby infringing the law of love was by claiming a divine right for the

A LETTER TO A HINDU

rulers: the Tsars, Sultans, Rajahs, Shahs, and other heads of states. But the longer humanity lived the weaker grew the belief in this peculiar, God—given right of the ruler. That belief withered in the same way and almost simultaneously in the Christian and the Brahman world, as well as in Buddhist and Confucian spheres, and in recent times it has so faded away as to prevail no longer against man's reasonable understanding and the true religious feeling. People saw more and more clearly, and now the majority see quite clearly, the senselessness and immorality of subordinating their wills to those of other people just like themselves, when they are bidden to do what is contrary not only to their interests but also to their moral sense. And so one might suppose that having lost confidence in any religious authority for a belief in the divinity of potentates of various kinds, people would try to free themselves from subjection to it. But unfortunately not only were the rulers, who were considered supernatural beings, benefited by having the peoples in subjection, but as a result of the belief in, and during the rule of, these pseudodivine beings, ever larger and larger circles of people grouped and established themselves around them, and under an appearance of governing took advantage of the people. And when the old deception of a supernatural and God-appointed authority had dwindled away these men were only concerned to devise a new one which like its predecessor should make it possible to hold the people in bondage to a limited number of rulers.

IV

Children, do you want to know by what your hearts should be guided? Throw aside your longings and strivings after that which is null and void; get rid of your erroneous thoughts about happiness and wisdom, and your empty and insincere desires. Dispense with these and you will know Love. KRISHNA.

Be not the destroyers of yourselves. Arise to your true Being, and then you will have nothing to fear. KRISHNA.

New justifications have now appeared in place of the antiquated, obsolete, religious ones. These new justifications are just as inadequate as the old ones, but as they are new their futility cannot immediately be recognized by the majority of men. Besides this, those who enjoy power propagate these new sophistries and support them so skilfully that they seem irrefutable even to many of those who suffer from the oppression these theories seek to justify. These new justifications are termed 'scientific'. But by the term 'scientific' is understood just what was formerly understood by the term 'religious': just as formerly everything called 'religious' was held to be unquestionable simply because it was called religious, so now all that is called 'scientific' is held to be unquestionable. In the present case the obsolete religious justification of violence which consisted in the recognition of the supernatural personality of the God-ordained ruler ('there is no power but of God') has been superseded by the 'scientific' justification which puts forward, first, the assertion that because the coercion of man by man has existed in all ages, it follows that such coercion must continue to exist. This assertion that people should continue to live as they have done throughout past ages rather than as their reason and conscience indicate, is what 'science' calls 'the historic law'. A further 'scientific' justification lies in the statement that as among plants and wild beasts there is a constant struggle for existence which always results in the survival of the fittest, a similar struggle should be carried on among human beings—beings, that is, who are gifted with intelligence and love; faculties lacking in the creatures subject to the struggle for existence and survival of the fittest. Such is the second 'scientific' justification.

The third, most important, and unfortunately most widespread justification is, at bottom, the age-old religious one just a little altered: that in public life the suppression of some for the protection of the majority cannot be avoided—so that coercion is unavoidable however desirable reliance on love alone might be in human intercourse. The only difference in this justification by pseudo-science consists in the fact that, to the question why such and such people and not others have the right to decide against whom violence may and must be used, pseudo-science now gives a different reply to that given by religion—which declared that the right to decide was valid because it was pronounced by persons possessed of divine power. 'Science' says that these decisions represent the will of the people, which under a constitutional form of government is supposed to find expression in all the decisions and actions of those who are at the helm at the moment.

Such are the scientific justifications of the principle of coercion. They are not merely weak but absolutely invalid, yet they are so much needed by those who occupy privileged positions that they believe in them as blindly as they formerly believed in the immaculate conception, and propagate them just as confidently. And the unfortunate majority of men bound to toil is so dazzled by the pomp with which these 'scientific truths' are presented, that under this new influence it accepts these scientific stupidities for holy truth, just as it formerly accepted the pseudo-religious justifications; and it continues to submit to the present holders of power who are just as hard-hearted but rather more numerous than before.

V

Who am I? I am that which thou hast searched for since thy baby eyes gazed wonderingly upon the world, whose horizon hides this real life from thee. I am that which in thy heart thou hast prayed for, demanded as thy birthright, although thou hast not known what it was. I am that which has lain in thy soul for hundreds and thousands of years. Sometimes I lay in thee grieving because thou didst not recognize me; sometimes I raised my head, opened my eyes, and extended my arms calling thee either tenderly and quietly, or strenuously, demanding that thou shouldst rebel against the iron chains which bound thee to the earth.
KRISHNA.

So matters went on, and still go on, in the Christian world. But we might have hope that in the immense Brahman, Buddhist, and Confucian worlds this new scientific superstition would not establish itself, and that the Chinese, Japanese, and Hindus, once their eyes were opened to the religious fraud justifying violence, would advance directly to a recognition of the law of love inherent in humanity, and which had been so forcibly enunciated by the great Eastern teachers. But what has happened is that the scientific superstition replacing the religious one has been accepted and secured a stronger and stronger hold in the East.

In your periodical you set out as the basic principle which should guide the actions of your people the maxim that: 'Resistance to aggression is not simply justifiable but imperative, nonresistance hurts both Altruism and Egotism.'

Love is the only way to rescue humanity from all ills, and in it you too have the only method of saving your people from enslavement. In very ancient times love was proclaimed with special strength and clearness among your people to be the religious basis of human life. Love, and forcible resistance to evil-doers, involve such a mutual contradiction as to destroy utterly the whole sense and meaning of the conception of love. And what follows? With a light heart and in the twentieth century you, an adherent of a religious people, deny their law, feeling convinced of your scientific enlightenment and your right to do so, and you repeat (do not take this amiss) the amazing stupidity indoctrinated in you by the advocates of the use of violence—the enemies of truth, the servants first of theology and then of science—your European teachers.

You say that the English have enslaved your people and hold them in subjection because the latter have not resisted resolutely enough and have not met force by force.

But the case is just the opposite. If the English have enslaved the people of India it is just because the latter recognized, and still recognize, force as the fundamental principle of the social order. In accord with that principle they submitted to their little rajahs, and on their behalf struggled against one another, fought the Europeans, the English, and are now trying to fight with them again.

A commercial company enslaved a nation comprising two hundred millions. Tell this to a man free from superstition and he will fail to grasp what these words mean. What does it mean that thirty thousand men, not athletes but rather weak and ordinary people, have subdued two hundred million vigorous, clever, capable, and freedom-loving people? Do not the figures make it clear that it is not the English who have enslaved the Indians, but the Indians who have enslaved themselves?

When the Indians complain that the English have enslaved them it is as if drunkards complained that the spirit-dealers who have settled among them have enslaved them. You tell them that they might give up drinking, but they reply that they are so accustomed to it that they cannot abstain, and that they must have alcohol to keep up their energy. Is it not the same thing with the millions of people who submit to thousands' or even to hundreds, of others—of their own or other nations?

If the people of India are enslaved by violence it is only because they themselves live and have lived by violence, and do not recognize the eternal law of love inherent in humanity.

Pitiful and foolish is the man who seeks what he already has, and does not know that he has it. Yes, Pitiful and foolish is he who does not know the bliss of love which surrounds him and which I have given him. KRISHNA.

As soon as men live entirely in accord with the law of love natural to their hearts and now revealed to them, which excludes all resistance by violence, and therefore hold aloof from all participation in violence—as soon as this happens, not only will hundreds be unable to enslave millions, but not even millions will be able to enslave a single individual. Do not resist the evil-doer and take no part in doing so, either in the violent deeds of the administration, in the law courts, the collection of taxes, or above all in soldiering, and no one in the world will be able to enslave you.

VI

O ye who sit in bondage and continually seek and pant for freedom, seek only for love. Love is peace in itself and peace which gives complete satisfaction. I am the key that opens the portal to the rarely discovered land where contentment alone is found. KRISHNA.

What is now happening to the people of the East as of the West is like what happens to every individual when he passes from childhood to adolescence and from youth to manhood. He loses what had hitherto guided his life and lives without direction, not having found a new standard suitable to his age, and so he invents all sorts of occupations, cares, distractions, and stupefactions to divert his attention from the misery and senselessness of his life. Such a condition may last a long time.

When an individual passes from one period of life to another a time comes when he cannot go on in senseless activity and excitement as before, but has to understand that although he has outgrown what before used to direct him, this does not mean that he must live without any reasonable guidance, but rather that he must formulate for himself an understanding of life corresponding to his age, and having elucidated it must be guided by it. And in the same way a similar time must come in the growth and development of humanity. I believe that such a time has now arrived—not in the sense that it has come in the year 1908, but that the inherent contradiction of human life has now reached an extreme degree of tension: on the one side there is the consciousness of the beneficence of the law of love, and on the other the existing order of life which has for centuries occasioned an empty, anxious, restless, and troubled mode of life, conflicting as it does with the law of love and built on the use of violence. This contradiction must be faced, and the solution will evidently not be favourable to the outlived law of violence, but to the truth which has dwelt in the hearts of men from remote antiquity: the truth that the law of love is in accord with the nature of man.

But men can only recognize this truth to its full extent when they have completely freed themselves from all religious and scientific superstitions and from all the consequent misrepresentations and sophistical distortions by which its recognition has been hindered for centuries.

To save a sinking ship it is necessary to throw overboard the ballast, which though it may once have been needed would now cause the ship to sink. And so it is with the scientific superstition which hides the truth of their welfare from mankind. In order that men should embrace the truth—not in the vague way they did in childhood, nor in the one-sided and perverted way presented to them by their religious and scientific teachers, but embrace it as their highest law—the complete liberation of this truth from all and every superstition (both pseudo-religious and pseudo-scientific) by which it is still obscured is essential: not a partial, timid attempt, reckoning with traditions sanctified by age and with the habits of the people—not such as was effected in the religious sphere by Guru-Nanak, the founder of the sect of the Sikhs, and in the Christian world by Luther, and by similar reformers in other religions—but a fundamental cleansing of religious consciousness from all ancient religious and modern scientific superstitions.

If only people freed themselves from their beliefs in all kinds of Ormuzds, Brahmas, Sabbaoths, and their incarnation as Krishnas and Christs, from beliefs in Paradises and Hells, in reincarnations and resurrections, from belief in the interference of the Gods in the external affairs of the universe, and above all, if they freed themselves from belief in the infallibility of all the various Vedas, Bibles, Gospels, Tripitakas, Korans, and the like, and also freed themselves from blind belief in a variety of scientific teachings about infinitely small atoms and molecules and in all the infinitely great and infinitely remote worlds, their movements and origin, as well as from faith in the infallibility of the scientific law to which humanity is at present subjected: the historic law,

128

the economic laws, the law of struggle and survival, and so on—if people only freed themselves from this terrible accumulation of futile exercises of our lower capacities of mind and memory called the 'Sciences', and from the innumerable divisions of all sorts of histories, anthropologies, homiletics, bacteriologics, jurisprudences, cosmographies, strategies—their name is legion—and freed themselves from all this harmful, stupifying ballast—the simple law of love, natural to man, accessible to all and solving all questions and perplexities, would of itself become clear and obligatory.

VII

Children, look at the flowers at your feet; do not trample upon them. Look at the love in your midst and do not repudiate it. KRISHNA.

There is a higher reason which transcends all human minds. It is far and near. It permeates all the worlds and at the same time is infinitely higher than they.

A man who sees that all things are contained in the higher spirit cannot treat any being with contempt.

For him to whom all spiritual beings are equal to the highest there can be no room for deception or grief.

Those who are ignorant and are devoted to the religious rites only, are in a deep gloom, but those who are given up to fruitless meditations are in a still greater darkness.

UPANISHADS, FROM VEDAS

Yes, in our time all these things must be cleared away in order that mankind may escape from self-inflicted calamities that have reached an extreme intensity. Whether an Indian seeks liberation from subjection to the English, or anyone else struggles with an oppressor either of his own nationality or of another—whether it be a Negro defending himself against the North Americans; or Persians, Russians, or Turks against the Persian, Russian, or Turkish governments, or any man seeking the greatest welfare for himself and for everybody else—they do not need explanations and justifications of old religious superstitions such as have been formulated by your Vivekanandas, Baba Bharatis, and others, or in the Christian world by a number of similar interpreters and exponents of things that nobody needs; nor the innumerable scientific theories about matters not only unnecessary but for the most part harmful. (In the spiritual realm nothing is indifferent: what is not useful is harmful.) What are wanted for the Indian as for the Englishman, the Frenchman, the German, and the Russian, are not Constitutions and Revolutions, nor all sorts of Conferences and Congresses, nor the many ingenious devices for submarine navigation and aerial navigation, nor powerful explosives, nor all sorts of conveniences to add to the enjoyment of the rich, ruling classes; nor new schools and universities with innumerable faculties of science, nor an augmentation of papers and books, nor gramophones and cinematographs, nor those childish and for the most part corrupt stupidities termed art—but one thing only is needful: the knowledge of the simple and clear truth which finds place in every soul that is not stupefied by religious and scientific superstitions—the truth that for our life one law is valid—the law of love, which brings the highest happiness to every individual as well as to all mankind. Free your minds from those overgrown, mountainous imbecilities which hinder your recognition of it, and at once the truth will emerge from amid the pseudo-religious nonsense that has been smothering it: the indubitable, eternal truth inherent in man, which is one and the same in all the great religions of the world. It will in due time emerge and make its way to general recognition, and the nonsense that has obscured it will disappear of itself, and with it will go the evil from which humanity now suffers.

Children, look upwards with your beclouded eyes, and a world full of joy and love will disclose itself to you, a rational world made by My wisdom, the only real world. Then you will know what love has done with you, what love has bestowed upon you, what love demands from you. KRISHNA.

Yasnaya Polyana
December 14th, 1908